Change in Classroom Practice

Change in Classroom Practice

Edited by

Hilary Constable,
Steve Farrow
and
Jerry Norton

The Falmer Press

(A member of the Taylor & Francis Group)

London • Washington, D.C.

UK   The Falmer Press, 4 John St, London WC1N 2ET
USA   The Falmer Press, Taylor & Francis Inc., 1900 Frost Road, Suite 101, Bristol, PA 19007

First published 1994

A catalogue record for this book is available from the British Library

Library of Congress Cataloging-in-Publication Data are available on request

ISBN 075070 198 6 cased
ISBN 075070 199 4 paperback

Jacket design by Caroline Archer
10.5/12pt Garamond
by Graphicraft Typesetters Ltd, Hong Kong

Printed in Great Britain by Burgess Science Press, Basingstoke on paper which has a specified pH value on final paper manufacture of not less than 7.5 and is therefore 'acid free'.

Contents

Introduction: Change in Classroom Practice: The Need to Know

Hilary Constable

The school improvement context

Little is known about how classroom practice changes. Over the last two decades deliberate and determined steps have been made to improve schooling in the United Kingdom (UK), and yet the place of classroom practice, or the mechanisms by which it changes, remain largely un-remarked and un-researched. How is it that serious efforts to improve classroom practice work, and how do these changes result in differences in pupil learning? This book charts current developments in the practical business of changing classroom practice to make schools more effective.

At a common-sense level we are aware that change is not simply commanded, and we act in accordance with this understanding, so it is not generally expected that legislation or other direction is sufficient to cause change in classroom practice. Instead, changes are mediated through a wide range of support systems and in-service provision — staff development of one sort and another — in order to accelerate and direct the intended changes. The question of interest is not so much *whether* these support mechanisms deliver what is expected, as *how* can they be made to work most effectively. In order to facilitate changes to make schooling more effective, the mechanisms need to be understood.

Increasingly, a sharper view of the effects and impact of professional and organizational development activities has been called for, and tracking the effects of various efforts to improve practice is now a prominent part of the work of all educators and researchers of education.

From the point of view of this book the most pressing concern is uncertainty about how change in classroom practice takes place, hence the classroom has been chosen deliberately as the central arena for studying school improvement, for if change does not to some extent happen in, or at least pass through, classrooms, it is hard to see how schools may otherwise become more effective. Put another way, if pupils and students continue to have the same planned experiences, it is hard to see how their achievements can be different. It is clear that we need to know more about how classroom practice changes.

The contributions to this book shed light on the ways in which classroom practice changes. There are two aspects to this: the first is detecting the effects on classroom practice of the efforts made to improve schools and classrooms, and the second is to understand how classroom practice changes. These two aspects are interdependent — it makes no sense to describe and quantify impact alone — an understanding is needed of how the various mechanisms of support have (or fail to have) their effect. Similarly, it makes little sense to have a richly textured picture of the experience of professional and organizational development without some notion of its results and effects.

The research context

Until recently there has been little research which has directly attempted to study change in classroom practice, and what there is has often been the by-product of other work. However, although a direct examination of change in classroom practice is unusual, there is an abundance of work which might be described as 'nearby' and which provides both background and questions. A rough and ready way of drawing attention to the distinctive contribution of this book is to say that other work tends to look at *either* classroom practice *or* change *or* the evaluation of professional development activities, but not to bring these areas together. This book presents, through examples, the current state of research into change in classroom practice. The book shows authors breaking new ground both in terms of their substantive areas of concern and also their responses to the research challenge.

All students learn that what will be found out about a situation is dependent on the questions asked. Nowhere is this more evident than in the areas of inquiry which might be drawn on when investigating change in classroom practice. The repertoire of research approaches includes differences not merely in the research focus, but also in the stance taken concerning the relationship between research and action for improvement. Studies range from those which have emphasized orderly description as a necessary basis for understanding and thence improvement, to those which are more urgent and have emphasized learning from intervention.

Classroom observation studies, critical accounts of good practice, analyses of change and of schools, evaluation of INSET, and biography, as well as work on school effectiveness and on school development, all have something to offer, although none of them directly addresses change in classroom practice.

Studies of classroom practice in the UK have made strenuous efforts to make systematic observation of classrooms and have been fruitful in showing patterns and raising questions — see for instance the well-known Observational Research and Classroom Learning Evaluation (ORACLE) Project (Galton *et al.*, 1980; Galton and Simon, 1980; Simon and Willcocks, 1981; Galton and Willcocks, 1983) and similarly the work by Bennett *et al.* (1984). A particular strength of these studies has been the collection of evidence which has variously confirmed or refuted everyday expectations of practice. The importance of this is hard to overstate. Galton drew attention to the fact that so entrenched and erroneous was the view in secondary schools about what must be happening in primary schools that:

> Despite this research evidence, secondary schools have continued to believe the rhetoric concerning primary teaching methods so that the emphasis in the first year after transfer has been on revision of these 'basics' while taking it for granted that pupils were highly proficient in the range of skills required to pursue independent studies. After transfer pupils were re-taught how to add, subtract and divide. The more able pupils became bored and disillusioned while the slow learners were often confused by having to learn new methods and new terminology. (Galton, 1987, p. 86)

Although change is not addressed directly, these studies are a rich source of patterns and questions.

What counts as good classroom practice is not a given; it is permanently open to challenge and revision. Detailed access to this debate is provided by work in what might be described as the critical academic tradition. Here authors address good practice in one area or another, often a subject area. See for instance, Bentley and Watts (1989) on science; Orton (1987) on mathematics; Tann (1988) on topic work; Thomas (1992) on classroom teamwork, and Weigand (1992) on geography. These books are characterized by their attention to evidence and to rational, analytical argument. Commonly they draw on previous research, present some new work and draw attention to critical issues in practice. In this way, and even though the authors do not usually address the processes of changing directly, the work contains much for those interested in change to draw on. The writers obliquely address change in that they have something to say about good practice.

Research into the processes of change is an important source of insight for studies of classrooms. Studies of change have drawn extensively on studies of complex, natural situations and contributions have centred on understanding the processes of change — see Fullan (1991), Fullan and Hargreaves (1992), Louis and Miles (1992), Huberman and Miles (1984). This work has offered a number of important ideas. The emphasis is on teachers and their context, and the relationships amongst teachers, leaders and administrators. These studies have drawn extensively on studies of complex and natural change situations. Fullan's analysis and synthesis of work on change discriminated educational change from organizational change; and understanding change from theories of how to change.

The earliest research into school effectiveness largely treated the classroom as a black box. In spite of this, the work provides an important context for research into classroom practice. Gray *et al.* (1990) Mortimore *et al.* (1988) and Reynolds (1992) all raise questions concerning the relationship between process and outcome in effective schools. More recent work has included a wider range of approaches under the title of school effectiveness, see, Anderson *et al.* 1989; Ramsay and Clark, 1990; Reynolds and Cuttance (1992) and some studies have also been able to take on classroom observation. Mortimore's study of junior school classrooms in the former Inner London Education Authority is one example where classroom observation was used as well as input and output measures. Here also the observation work drew on the earlier ORACLE project (Mortimore *et al.*, 1988).

Reynolds and Cuttance (1992) show the close interrelationship of research on school effectiveness with school development, and Badger's (1992) lucid account of changing a disruptive school shows the collection of evidence in the service of school improvement. Work in the area of school development is at the interface of action and research and has links with work on effectiveness and on change — see for instance, Caldwell and Spinks (1992), Constable *et al.* (1987, 1988), Dalin and Rust (1983), Loucks-Horsley and Hergert (1985), Loucks-Horsley *et al.* (1987), Holly and Southworth (1989). As these studies are at the interface of action and research there is need for readers to discriminate between those which deal largely with how things ought to work and those which describe how they do work.

In-service education for teachers (INSET) has been an important means by which change is mediated and there has been a strong tradition of evaluation linked with it, especially in the UK and amongst teacher educators (Lomax, 1989; Nixon, 1992; and Rudduck, 1986). This work has been generally rich in understanding the processes of change, but occasionally squeamish about outcomes and comparisons.

Halpin (1990) broke with tradition in their comparative survey of teachers' opinions. Constable and Long (1991) took this further to combine tracking the impact of in-service education with understanding the processes of change. With a more developmental slant, Joyce and Showers (1988) have made decisive claims about the way staff development can improve student achievement.

Another perspective on the array of influences acting on teachers has come from studies using biography (Clandinin, 1986; Goodson, 1992). These can provide insights into change in practice. Work which is essentially analytical is a further powerful source of understanding. For instance, Alexander (1984), Ball (1987), Bowe and Ball (1992) and Hoyle (1986) show the array of forces, sometimes contradictory, which work on teachers. Alexander's (1992) later work is notable in that it combines analysis and observation, and furthermore it directly addresses change and its relationship with in-service education, and includes observations of practice.

The challenge to research appropriately

Each of these approaches confers a distinctive shading, but neither individually nor together are these traditions sufficient to meet the challenge of detecting whether, and understanding how, classroom practice changes. Change in classroom practice is an area of research which is not adequately covered by other approaches, therefore some thought about how it is to be tackled as a research question is necessary.

Researching change in practice presents methodological challenges. The basic question can be stated baldly enough — What causes what? — but in this form it is not accessible to research. All researchers know that to detect and record change is not the same thing as to identify the forces causing change. This knowledge is of little relief when the question of greatest interest is indeed 'What causes what?'.

Research into change needs an authentic relationship with everyday understandings, including some thought about the time frame and visibility. Researchers differ in their stance about the place of teachers and researchers in their work and it needs to be remembered that not only change but also its research takes place in a political and social arena.

What is wanted is knowledge of whether initiatives have had the effects intended, but experience tells us that the questions are unlikely to be so simple in practice. Change does not either happen or not happen. It is rare for nothing to happen, but common for changes to work out rather differently from those expected or intended. Sometimes, changes proposed appear to have a much smaller impact than might have been expected at their inception. The issue here is one of magnitude: the change is simply much too small or too slow. Other changes appear to lose focus or direction: those changes which do not work out in the way expected or which don't achieve what was intended, but something else instead. The 'something else' may be no worse than the original idea, it may be better, but somehow change appears to have taken place at right angles. It is these more mildly puzzling initiatives as much as spectacular failures or successes that remind us that whilst there is a considerable body of knowledge about change, there is not yet sufficient sophistication to turn this into means of getting change to happen. It is this practical application which drives the need to understand how change takes place, as well as to record its occurrence.

The focus of attention for studies of change needs active definition and is at the same time somewhat problematic. If a study is to make a contribution to what is known through systematic study then it must focus on something rather than on everything. At the same time, understanding 'What causes what?' requires an effort to understand multidimensional relationships.

It is possible to attend to the situation in a number of ways. Teachers, pupils, classroom organization, events, interaction or learning outcomes are each possible as a focus for attention. The issue of what counts as data and what is noise is significant in the design of each piece of research to be reported. The important point here is that it is not a foregone conclusion as to where attention should be directed. Neither is the decision apolitical: it results from the views of each researcher not only about what counts as desirable practice and change, but also about what counts as research. This is especially evident in the place given to teachers in relation both to practice and to research.

The very nature of change itself provides a challenge to researchers. Direct techniques such as longitudinal studies and time sampling can be used to detect change. What is much less clear, funding apart, is how to choose an informative time frame. Taken over time, a new practice may first appear and later disappear. On its own, such an observation may not be very informative. One reason for the disappearance may be because the practice has ceased. At the other extreme, another reason may be because the practice was such a success it has become incorporated into everyday practice and is no longer separately identifiable: it has become part of the way things are done. A new practice may be rejected, and like an organ transplant, often after some considerable time has elapsed when all appeared to be well, or, new practices can be lost simply through attrition.

The tale of the Schools Council Impact and Take-Up Project makes salutary reading for researchers of change. Steadman *et al.* (1981) found, when they looked at the extent to which Schools Council Projects had had an impact on teachers' practice, that they had to remain doubtful about the findings. Briefly, the reason lay not in the miserable lack of impact but in the fact that projects could not be identified by teachers. The materials had been sold under individual titles and the methods had not been marketed as Schools Council, but rather as good practice. Consequently, it was hard to identify the routes of influence because the projects were, so to speak, inadequately tagged.

> So great was this problem of identification that the questionnaire listings had to give prominence to as many of the published series and book titles as possible. Project names could not be reliably linked to their output by teachers. (Steadman *et al.*, 1981, p. 45)

In relation to change in classroom practice, teachers find themselves both actors and acted upon. Teachers especially, but also others involved in change are not neutral: they have values in relation to both teaching and research. They shape the situation and at the same time they are shaped by the situation in which they find themselves. Incorporating the place of actors into research remains problematic.

Actual changes designed to improve the achievements of pupils and the effectiveness of schools are not conjured instantaneously by legislation or, for that matter, in any other way. However, change is political, and so is its research. On each matter there are those who wish to demonstrate progress and those whose interest lies in demonstrating the opposite. In the same way that teachers can be seen as actors and as the object of actions, researchers carry out their work in the world and are not neutral figures. In this respect at least, researchers are also actors. Educational researchers can be decidedly poor in negotiating the significance of their findings with their audiences, sometimes believing that the findings will speak for themselves.

As in other areas, studies of classrooms are under pressure to come up with 'best-buy' strategies and preferably fail-safe ones at that. Attempts simply to understand are pressed to produce prescriptions and even magic potions. Researchers need well-developed skills in negotiating with their audiences what can be said and considered well founded and what is speculative and should be treated with care. There is a complementary challenge resulting from studies which start from a 'best buy'. Some studies start essentially as a check on the good effects of a practice in which the researchers are believers. It is not impossible to come up with powerful insights from studies with such a beginning, but it is decidedly difficult. Commitment to a specific form of revised practice is a risky position for a researcher — they need to hold on to their skills in noticing uncomfortable findings.

Investigating change in classroom practice

The research and development work in this book reports how a variety of initiatives to improve practice come to influence practice. The contributors break new ground and offer creative solutions to this challenge and sometimes make controversial claims about the way forward. Each of the contributors presents discoveries about the ways in which classroom practice has been changed or challenged by deliberate efforts to improve schooling.

The chapters which follow are united by their concentration on change in classroom practice rather than change *or* classroom practice *or* professional development. They draw on a spectrum of traditions and bring together analytical and empirical work. In these chapters there is an emphasis on implementation, rather than planning, and a range of possible ways forward is suggested. However, these chapters do not all possess the same point of view. Different definitions of the research problem offer a richness of voices, not only about change, but also about research. Implicitly or explicitly, each researcher takes a stance not only about what constitutes desirable practice and change, but also about what counts as research. The implied or stated view in each study about what counts as good practice affects not only the interpretation of findings but also the design and implementation of the study.

The differing perspectives provide complementary views but it is not true to say that as yet they can be woven together evenly or synthesized smoothly. It would be more truthful to say that although each of these studies attempts in some way to colonize new ground and to study change in classroom practice there are creative tensions amongst them. A more direct way of putting this is with the image of crashing gears or grating paradigms. The different stances clash against each other. On good days more light than heat is generated.

What is clear and refreshing from these studies is that careful observation quickly generates hypotheses and insights which can be pursued. It is exciting that from these pieces of work which grapple with methodological problems of some magnitude come insights with an authentic ring.

References

ALEXANDER, R.J. (1984) *Primary Teaching*, London, Holt, Rinehart and Winston.

ALEXANDER, R.J. (1992) *Policy and Practice in Primary Education*, London, Routledge.

ANDERSON, L.W., RYAN, D.W. and SHAPIRO, B.J. (1989) *The IEA Classroom Environment Study*, Oxford, Pergamon.

BADGER, B. (1992) 'Changing a Disruptive School', in REYNOLDS, D. and CUTTANCE, P. *School Effectiveness, Research, Policy and Practice*, London, Cassell.

BALL, S.J. (1987) *The Micro-Politics of the School: Towards a Theory of School Organisation*, London, Methuen.

BENNETT, N., DESFORGES, C., COCKBURN, A. and WILKINSON, B. (1984) *The Quality of Pupil Learning Experiences*, London, Lawrence Erlbaum.

BENTLEY, D. and WATTS, M. (1989) *Learning and Teaching in School Science: Practical Alternatives*, Milton Keynes, Open University Press.

BOWE, R. and BALL, S.J. (1992) *Reforming Education and Changing Schools*, London, Routledge.

CALDERHEAD, J. (1988) (Ed.) *Teachers' Professional Learning*, London, The Falmer Press.

CALDWELL, B.J. and SPINKS, J.M. (1992) *Leading the Self-Managing School*, London, The Falmer Press.

CERVERO, R.M. (1988) *Effective Continuing Education for Professionals*, London, Jossey-Bass.

CLANDININ, D.J. (1986) *Classroom Practice: Teacher Images in Action*, London, The Falmer Press.

CONSTABLE, H., WILLIAMS, R., BROWN, R., LUDLOW, R. and TAGGART, L. (1987) *An Evaluation of GRIDS in Leeds*, School of Education, University of Leeds.

CONSTABLE, H., BROWN, R. and WILLIAMS, R. (1988) 'An Evaluation of the Implementation of GRIDS in one Local Education Authority', *Educational Management and Administration*, **16**, 1.

CONSTABLE, H. and LONG, A.F. (1991) 'Changing Science Teaching: Lessons from a Long-Term Evaluation of a Short In-Service Course', *International Journal of Science Education*, **13**, 4, pp. 405–419.

DALIN, P. and RUST, V.D. (1983) *Can Schools Learn?*, Windsor, NFER-Nelson.

ELLIOTT, J. (1991) *Action Research for Educational Change*, Milton Keynes, Open University Press.

FULLAN, M.G. (1991) *The New Meaning of Educational Change*, London, Cassell.

FULLAN, M. and HARGREAVES, A. (Eds.) (1992) *Teacher Development and Educational Change*, London, The Falmer Press.

GALTON, M. (1987) 'Change and Continuity in the Primary School: The research evidence', *Oxford Review of Education*, **13**, 1, pp. 81–93.

GALTON, M., SIMON, B. and CROLL, P. (1980) *Inside the Primary Classroom*, London, Routledge and Kegan Paul.

GALTON, M. and SIMON B. (Eds.) (1980) *Progress and Performance in the Primary Classroom*, London, Routledge and Kegan Paul.

GALTON, M. and WILLCOCKS, J. (Eds.) (1983) *Moving from the Primary Classroom*, London, Routledge and Kegan Paul.

GOODSON, I.F. (1992) *Studying Teachers' Lives*, London, Routledge and Kegan Paul.

GRAY, J., JESSON, D. and SIME, N. (1990) 'Estimating the differences in the examination performances of secondary schools in six LEAs: A multilevel approach to school effectiveness', *Oxford Review of Education*, **16**, 2, pp. 137–58.

HALPIN, D. (1990) 'Teachers' Perceptions of the Effects of In-Service Education', *British Educational Research Journal*, **16**, 2, pp. 163–77.

HOLLY, P. and SOUTHWORTH, G. (1989) *The Developing School*, London, The Falmer Press.

HOYLE, E. (1986) *The Politics of School Management*, London, Hodder and Stoughton.

HUBERMAN, A.M. and MILES, M.B. (1984) *Innovation Up Close*, New York, Plenum.

JOYCE, B. and SHOWERS, B. (1988) *Student Achievement through Staff Development*, London, Longman.

LOMAX, P. (Ed.) (1989) *The Management of Change*, BERA Dialogues, Clevedon, Multilingual Matters.

LOUCKS-HORSLEY, S. and HERGERT, L.F. (1985) *An Action Guide to School Improvement*, Andover, Massachusetts, Association for Supervision and Curriculum Development.

LOUCKS-HORSLEY, S., HARDING, C.K., ARBUCKLE, M.A., MURRAY, L.B., DUBEA, C. and WILLIAMS, M.K. (1987) *Continuing to Learn: A Guidebook for Teacher Development*, Massachusetts, The Regional Laboratory for Educational Improvement of the Northeast and Islands and National Staff Development Council.

LOUIS, K.S. and MILES, M.B. (1992) *Improving the Urban High School: What Works and Why*, London, Cassell.

MORTIMORE, P., SAMMONS, P., STOLL, L., LEWIS, D. and ECOB, R. (1988) *School Matters: The Junior Years*, London, Open Books.

NIXON, J. (1992) *Evaluating the Whole Curriculum*, Milton Keynes, Open University Press.

ORTON, A. (1987) *Learning Mathematics: Issues, Theory and Classroom Practice*, London, Cassell.

RAMSAY, W. and CLARK, E.E. (1990) *New Ideas for Effective School Improvement: Vision, Social Capital, Evaluation*, London, The Falmer Press.

REYNOLDS, D. (1992) 'School Effectiveness and School Improvement: An Updated Review of the British Literature', in REYNOLDS, D. and CUTTANCE, P. *School Effectiveness, Research, Policy and Practice*, London, Cassell.

REYNOLDS, D. and CUTTANCE, P. (1992) *School Effectiveness, Research, Policy and Practice*, London, Cassell.

RUDDUCK, J. (1986) 'Curriculum change; management or meaning?' *School Organisation*, **6**, 1, pp. 107–114.

SIMON, B. and WILLCOCKS, J. (Eds.) (1981) *Research and Practice in the Primary Classroom*, London, Routledge and Kegan Paul.

STEADMAN, S.D., PARSONS, C., LILLIE, K. and SALTER, B. (1981) *The Schools Council: Its Take-Up in Schools and General Impact: A Final Report*, London, Schools Council Publications.

TANN, S. (Ed.) (1988) *Developing Topic Work in the Primary School*, London, The Falmer Press.

THOMAS, G. (1992) *Effective Classroom Teamwork: Support or Intrusion?* London, Routledge and Kegan Paul.

WEIGAND, P. (1992) *Places in the Primary School*, London, The Falmer Press.

Part 1

Theoretical Assumptions and Methodological Decisions

Part 1   Theoretical Assumptions and Methodological Decisions

In the first section the writers have placed an emphasis on one or another theoretical position. They have set out how their thinking about change in the classroom has influenced the construction of their various researches.

Cooper and McIntyre argue the need to get right inside the problem and to construct understandings. They propose three starting points: teachers' craft knowledge, pupils' learning strategies and curriculum change. Cooper and McIntyre point out that in principle these areas complement each other and go on to isolate key issues arising from each of the three source sets. They draw attention to the need to surface, understand and relate different perspectives; and the need to understand the relationship of different strands of teachers' knowledge to the change process. They wish to understand how pupils construe their own learning in relation to what teachers do, or try to do, or think they are doing. Characteristically, they are concerned with authenticity as opposed to plausibility: a tall order bearing in mind the challenge they have set themselves.

Adey sets out his theoretical position forcefully. For him the issue is one of outcomes. Pupil learning outcomes are the central concern, and interventions either raise these or they do not. He argues for the evaluation of INSET in terms of the achievement of pupils and suggests that this can be achieved rather more easily than is often made out. He goes on to outline how, starting from a specific innovation, a simple experimental design can demonstrate impact (or not) on pupil learning. His argument is important in that it combines a concern for pupil learning with an interest in one of the principal vectors of change: in-service education for teachers. Adey's work is challenging in the way he has decided to deal with complexity, essentially he steps round it and has treated the situation as straightforward.

Kinder and Harland also use the evaluation of INSET as the basis for their work. They wish to identify and demonstrate the conditions under which INSET precipitates change in classroom practice. They, like McIntyre and Cooper, are interested in ordering complexity and are curious to understand how, where there has been little impact on classroom practice, the INSET process has broken down. Kinder and Harland have constructed and developed through two research projects a new typology and hierarchy of INSET outcomes. Their work is consistent with earlier attempts to provide an analysis of outcomes, in that effects in the classroom are dependent on other outcomes of INSET. However, Kinder and Harland take a step beyond previous attempts to order and organize the outcomes of INSET. Their hierarchy responds to a more organizationally focused INSET provision and combines a variety of different sorts of outcome. They draw attention to the poverty of much in-house in-service work, not so much in its delivery but rather in the planning. The authors argue that for change in classroom practice to occur, outcomes at each different level must be planned, they will not come about by chance. The typology can help with focusing planning.

This section might best be thought of as consisting of explanations through examples of ways of organizing research about change in classroom practice. The strong theoretical interest shown has not removed the need for these authors to devise research methods which can be used, and which are robust enough to inform those whose work is concerned with making classroom practice more effective. The contrasts are striking: Cooper and McIntyre have tried to get inside the complexities of change in classroom practice whereas Adey has cut through the complexities by treating the situation as if it were straightforward, and Kinder and Harland have imposed a pragmatic order. The overt exploration of theoretical position in these three chapters provides a powerful illustration of the way that researchers' thinking about the substantive matters has influenced the construction of their research.

1 Researching Teachers' and Pupils' Classroom Strategies

Paul Cooper and Donald McIntyre

Change in classroom practice is interesting for many reasons. The reasons and causes for classroom change, the kinds of change which are possible in classrooms, and the processes by which such changes can come about are all important for anyone concerned that schooling should contribute effectively to young people's education. Equally, however, change in classroom practice, and whether it does or does not happen when teachers or others want it to happen, is interesting because of what it can tell us about the nature of classroom practice.

This chapter reports on the early stages of a research project which is concerned with current changes in classroom practice both out of interest in the nature and processes of these changes, and also with a view to understanding better the nature of teachers' and pupils' classroom practices, especially those which they themselves believe to be effective.

The project as a whole is concerned with developing understandings which will be of long-term strategic importance for the development of schooling including current policy-led changes. We shall present the theoretical issues which underline the project and the methodological and practical concerns to which we have had to give attention. In this chapter we will not be reporting findings.

Rationale for the project

This study of classroom practice has three main complementary concerns: teachers' professional craft knowledge, pupils' classroom learning strategies, and the impact of the National Curriculum on subject teaching in the early years of secondary schooling.

Teachers' professional craft knowledge

Viewing teachers' expertise as professional craft knowledge has been both actively promoted and strongly resisted on both sides of the Atlantic in recent years. In three seminal papers in the *British Journal of Teacher Education*, Desforges and McNamara (1977; 1979; McNamara and Desforges, 1978) argued the case that we should seek for understandings of effective teaching not primarily through academic philosophy or social science but rather through gaining access to the complex, subtle and purposeful judgments made by experienced teachers in their classroom practice, and by subjecting such professional craft knowledge, as they describe it, to critical examination. In the United States, Tom (1984) wrote about the elaborate knowledge and intellectual demands of the 'moral craft' of teaching. Objections to this way of thinking have come largely from those (e.g. House and Lapan, 1989) who view 'craft' as rather mechanical and wish to emphasize the artistry of teaching at its best. Taking a view rather of craft incorporating artistry, Brown and McIntyre (1992) sought to gain access to, and to describe, the professional craft knowledge of sixteen teachers working in primary and secondary schools and, among the latter, in different subject areas. One of their reasons for being interested in such knowledge was that, like Desforges and McNamara, they believed in its potential importance for initial teacher education. Another, however, was that their previous research on innovations in classrooms (e.g. Brown and McIntyre, 1982) had persuaded them that significant changes in teachers' classroom practices were only possible or desirable if the craft knowledge teachers were already using was first understood.

In their research on teachers' professional craft knowledge, Brown and McIntyre found that all the teachers they worked with drew in their classroom practice on rich, sophisticated and apparently very individual knowledge. They were able to describe common features of this knowledge, but only in rather abstract terms, concerned for example with the nature of the goals sought, the repertoires of actions available and the kinds of factors of which account was taken. They were persuaded, too, that the kind of knowledge being revealed to them was both very valuable and also not previously systematically described.

A major concern of the present project, therefore, is to continue this exploration of teachers' professional craft knowledge. The aspiration now, however, is to do this in a more focused way. What kinds of professional craft knowledge are available for specific purposes within relatively circumscribed contexts? So we are working with English teachers and History teachers, working within the framework of the National Curriculum, in Year 7 in the first instance, and we are focusing especially on the professional craft knowledge used by the teachers

(a)   in making their subjects accessible to their pupils; and
(b)   in catering for differences among their pupils.

As will be explained, trying to focus on particular areas of professional craft knowledge raises new difficulties.

Pupils' classroom learning strategies

Our second perspective on classroom practice in principle complements the first. If it is important to understand the classroom thinking which underlies teachers' successful classroom practice, it is surely equally important to understand the classroom thinking which underlies pupils' successful classroom practice. If teachers need sophisticated skills to teach effectively, is it not likely that pupils also need skills to learn effectively in classrooms? If researchers have, as we would suggest, previously failed to take adequate account of teachers' perspectives in our attempts to describe their classroom expertise, how much more have we failed to take account of pupils' classroom perspectives, and especially those which underlie their successful attempts to learn in classrooms?

What previous work we could most fruitfully build on was less obvious in this aspect of the research. Three important reviews of research on pupils' perspectives and strategies in classrooms have been important for us. Much of the relevant British research is synthesized by Woods (1990). In his introduction, Woods comments that:

> Schools . . . are places of struggle . . . Schools are also places of learning . . . This present book is addressed to the learning aspects (pp. vii–viii).

Very little of this very interesting book, however, is about the learning which pupils attempt to do, or the strategies which they adopt for learning. Most of it — fairly reflecting, we believe, the research which has been reported — is about pupils' relationships with teachers, fellow-pupils and the ways they deal with the demands of schools. Even in the chapter on 'Pupils at Work', Woods has to report that 'The pupils' approach to schoolwork has been less commonly researched' (p. 158).

Another review that has been of importance to us is that by Weinstein and Mayer (1986) on 'The Teaching of Learning Strategies'. It has been interesting to learn from this review about ways in which classroom learning strategies have been construed by educators, and about how far and under what conditions pupils have been responsive to the strategies teachers have tried to teach them. The conceptualization of the strategies however, is in terms of what pupils were taught, not in terms of how they experienced and used them.

Most helpful has been the research review by Wittrock (1986), whose thinking is closest to our own in that he is concerned with 'at least two . . . links between teaching and student achievement. The first link is between teaching and student cognition. The second link is between student cognition and learning or achievement' (p. 297). He reviews many studies which offer interesting theoretical perspectives on pupils' classroom thinking and their learning strategies and also valuable ideas about procedures for studying pupils' classroom cognitions. All of these studies, however, have relied upon prior theoretical frameworks in terms of which pupils' classroom experiences, thought processes or learning strategies could be described and analyzed. In our investigation, we want to understand how pupils themselves construe their learning, especially their successful learning, in classrooms, how they describe their successful efforts at learning, and why they set about learning as they do. Just as with the teachers, we make no presuppositions as to how pupils might construe learning successes or their ways of attaining these successes. In particular, we make no assumptions about how these will be related to what teachers are trying to do. We shall, of course, be very interested in how teachers' and pupils' efforts, perceptions and thinking are related, and in how they perceive each others' efforts as facilitating their own successes or as not doing so.

The impact of the National Curriculum

Our third major concern is with the impact of the National Curriculum, with all the force of its legal national status and of the assessment and reporting sanctions associated with it, on classroom teaching, as teachers themselves perceive it. The specific effects it has on English and History teaching will themselves be interesting. At a more general theoretical level, however, we are concerned with the interacting effects of this imposed innovation at two levels. At the ideological level, how will teachers with different subject ideologies of English or History accommodate to the requirement to teach the National Curriculum's programmes of study and attainment targets; and how will teachers with different ideologies relating to differences among pupils accommodate to the requirements to assess pupils, and to report assessment in terms of the specified levels of attainment? As the work of Ball and Bowe (1990) suggests, intellectual stances and social processes within subject departments may be important here. And at the level of classroom practice, how far and in what ways will teachers find it necessary and possible to change well established classroom teaching strategies? How will accommodations and resistances at the classroom practice level influence or be influenced by accommodations and resistances at the ideological level?

These then are our primary concerns. At the heart of the research is the task of gaining access to teachers' professional craft knowledge and to pupils' classroom learning craft knowledge, and that of exploring relationships between what teachers and pupils see themselves as doing. The approach used is a development of that used by Brown and McIntyre

(1992) with, in most respects and so far as can be judged, considerable success. But the new tasks bring with them distinctive problems and,
perhaps, distinctive opportunities.

Problems of researching pupils' and teachers' classroom strategies

To a large extent the nature of our research questions defines for us the
research approach that we must adopt. Because we want to understand
teaching and learning from the viewpoint of teachers and pupils, we must
avoid the importation of our own presuppositions into the research setting,
by adopting a strategy which enables our subjects to reveal their authentic
perceptions of teaching and learning. However, central to our study is the
intention to direct our subjects' attention to particular realms of their experience. This prescriptive dimension introduces an element of tension which
has to be accounted for in our research design and procedures.

Methodological problems

There are three broad categories of problem that need to be addressed in
a study of the present type. The first category deals with the fundamental
viability of research which claims to report subjects' accurate recall of
cognitive processes; it poses the question:

- are the cognitive processes that underlie the skilled behaviour of
  teachers and learners available to conscious reflection?

The second category refers to the problematic relationship that necessarily
exists between the researcher and his/her subjects. In research of this type,
the researcher treads a fine line between, on the one hand, allowing subjects to be expansive, and on the other seeking results, in the form of
answers to research questions. The key difficulties here are:

- how can the researcher successfully motivate subjects to put the
  necessary time and effort into revealing their authentic thoughts
  and concerns?
- how can the researcher deal with the possibility that subjects might
  present merely plausible as opposed to authentic responses?

The third category of problems again highlights the tension between the
researcher's desire to answer specific questions and the necessity to be as
non-directive as possible. The particular difficulty, in the context of the
present project, is that if pupils and teachers focus on entirely different
classroom events and behaviours in their personal accounts, how are we
going to develop an understanding of (for example) the particular effects
on pupils of what their teacher perceives to be an important teaching

strategy? Clearly, to prescribe that the focus of teacher-pupil perceptions should be on events selected by the researcher would contravene the major intention of seeking out teacher and pupil perceptions. The chief problem here, therefore, is

- in the absence of spontaneous commonality of teacher and pupil perceptions of significant classroom events, how might it be possible for the researcher to engineer such commonality, without influencing or interfering with the flow of subjects' spontaneous reports of their perceptions?

Each of these types of problems will now be dealt with in greater detail, along with some of the proposed solutions.

The validity of verbal reports of classroom cognitions

Are the cognitions which inform the skilled activities of teachers and learners available to conscious recall?

There is a substantial body of research into teachers' thinking which suggests that much of what expert teachers do in the classroom takes the form of intuitive, almost automatic, judgments and actions, developed over many years of experience (e.g. Olson, 1984; Johnston, 1988). Leinhardt (1988) argues that much of the knowledge on which such judgments and actions depend is 'situated' in distinctive types of classroom context, rather than being of an abstract context-free variety; and other researchers, such as Shulman (1986) have suggested that teachers' craft knowledge takes the form of 'case knowledge', based on recollections of entire classroom episodes. It seems that experienced teachers may 'recognize' classroom situations as being similar to others previously encountered and, without consciously articulating to themselves the needs, the possibilities or the reasons, intuitively 'know' what they consider it most appropriate to do.

If this is anything like a correct understanding, will teachers be able to recall or reconstruct the cognitions informing their successful classroom activities? Brown and McIntyre (1992), confronting the same issue, found it necessary to make an important distinction in answering this question. They found that, with help and with effort, teachers could report some hours later what they believed to be, and what persuasively appeared to be, valid accounts of the ways they had seen classroom situations and acted in them; thus they could recall what they saw happening which they liked or didn't like, what factors in the situations seemed important to them, what they wanted to achieve, and why the actions which they took seemed appropriate. On the other hand, quite consistently they seemed unable to recall their own cognitive processes, such as the ways in which their perceptions of situations developed, alternative courses of action which they considered, and their decision-making processes. Brown and McIntyre

(1992) suggest that the attention which experienced teachers have to give to the complex external situations which face them during classroom teaching leaves them with little time to monitor their own cognitive processes. Furthermore, such monitoring seems irrelevant to the ways in which teachers judge how to act.

The extent of pupils' awareness of their learning processes is a slightly less problematic area. There is evidence from a wide range of sources to suggest that pupils are capable of describing cognitive processes they claim to employ in learning. However, the literature suggests that the facility to make such reports tends to be related to pupils' measured ability, to success in learning, and to the conscious adoption of strategies for learning. Research reviewed by Wittrock (1986) and Wang (1990) indicates that there is a close relationship between school achievement and students' perceptions of the degree to which they are able to exert control over the learning process. Not only do students who perceive themselves to have a high degree of control over their learning tend to succeed as learners, but pupils with learning difficulties who are trained to develop an increased sense of personal control over their learning, tend to experience improvements in their level of recorded achievement (Wang and Walberg, 1983). Research by Biggs (1987), which suggests a link between student motivation and choice of learning strategy, supports this view. Anderson (1981), Peterson and Swing (1982), and Winne and Marx (1982), also provide evidence of pupils consciously employing cognitive strategies, which they are able to report.

On the face of it, then, it might seem that at least some pupils appear to offer us a more promising source of information about the cognitive processes involved in classroom learning than their teachers offer for the cognitive processes of teaching. If this is correct, a possible reason for this state of affairs might be that where pupils reveal this facility it is as a result of teachers instructing pupils in the area of learning strategies. Therefore, whilst pupils learn to manipulate their cognitive processes as an important skill for successful classroom learning, the process of learning to teach in classrooms seems to involve cognitive processes becoming more automatic and less consciously controlled.

There is some reason to believe, however, that the conditions of the present project may make it possible to gain access to some of the teachers', as well as pupils', thought processes. Although skilled teaching involves a great deal of judgment of an automatized kind, teachers are often faced with the need to adapt to variations in their working contexts (Doyle, 1977; Clark, 1986), or in the wider policy context as it affects their own schools and departments (Ball and Bowe, 1990). Confronted with new demands and conditions, teachers may draw more consciously on knowledge and experience in order to devise appropriate responses; and this in turn may make their 'sense making' processes more accessible. A helpful parallel from a very different kind of study is offered by Hargreaves *et al.*'s

(1975) study of teachers' roles in the social construction of pupil deviance. They found that the processes by which teachers perceived individual pupils were virtually inaccessible to researchers by the time the pupils had reached their third year of secondary school. In order to access the processes of teachers' perceptions of pupils, the researchers had to investigate these during the formative periods when teachers were coming to terms with the pupils in the first two years of secondary schooling.

In this project, the conditions of particular importance are those related to the advent of the National Curriculum in secondary English and History. In so far as teachers need to re-examine the appropriateness of aspects of their craft knowledge for these new circumstances, and to develop new strategies or to take account of new factors or criteria, their cognitive processes in planning and conducting their teaching may be more deliberate and conscious and therefore more accessible to us. Furthermore, concentrating the study on the first year of secondary schooling will pose for teachers and pupils situations in which their sense making processes, as they come to terms with each other, will be at their most active.

Field relations

Having explored the general viability of the enterprise, and the conditions under which the data we seek is likely to be most readily available, the next issue to be dealt with concerns the manner in which the study is to be conducted. Of central importance here is the nature and quality of the relationships that the researcher develops with the subjects of the study ('field relations'). How can the researcher successfully motivate subjects to put the necessary time and effort into revealing their authentic thoughts and concerns?

First of all it is important to clarify claims we hope to make about the data we propose to collect. A keyword here is 'authentic'. We want our subjects to share with us their authentic understanding of factors which they experience as having an influence on the quality of teaching and learning in the classrooms we are studying.

Second, we must acknowledge the demands that our interactions place on our subjects. Whilst sense making processes are central to teachers' and pupils' normal activities the articulation of these processes is far more important on the researcher agenda than on the teacher or pupil agenda. Furthermore, this articulation process is both demanding in terms of the difficulties involved, and potentially threatening to those who worry that they might expose possible weaknesses in their thinking.

In order to overcome the difficulties of motivation, the researchers presented the project from the outset as being based on the idea that experienced teachers and pupils are in possession of extensive and complex knowledge which enables them to engage in effective teaching and learning. The criteria for 'effectiveness' and the meaning of the term 'learning' are themselves part of this knowledge, as is the means by which these are achieved. The researcher's role, therefore, is to stimulate teachers and pupils to recall and describe this knowledge. The researcher's role is quite distinct from that of the teacher and pupil and does not place him in a position to judge teacher or pupil. In this sense the teacher and the pupils are cast as the unrivalled experts in their own fields.

Not only are teachers and pupils cast in the role of experts, but also it is what they have done well that the researcher asks them to recall and to describe. Although pupils and especially teachers frequently do talk in the interviews about things which did not go well, it is through consistently emphasizing his interest in what they do well and what has been successful in their teaching and learning, that the researcher demonstrates his belief in their expertise and encourages them to reveal it.

Before formal approaches are made to head teachers, the heads of departments in selected schools are approached on an informal basis, with information about the project. Only after informal discussion with the department, and the clear indication that members of the department are interested in the project and willing to commit sufficient time to it, are the head teachers approached with a formal request to carry out the research.

Pupils present a slightly different set of problems from teachers, in that initial approaches to them are made via the teachers. This unfortunate necessity carries with it the hidden danger that the researcher may become associated in the minds of pupils with the authority structures of the school. In order to minimize this problem the researcher takes a number of measures designed to give pupils a sense of control over their involvement in the project. Before engaging in observation work with the pupils, the researcher must spend time mixing in a fairly informal way with pupils in lessons. Only once a degree of rapport has been established can the researcher invite pupils for interview. When a pupil is invited to interview, the voluntary nature of his/her participation can be stressed by allowing the pupil to select a day and time that is suitable to them (i.e. this necessarily involves breaktimes or lunchtimes); the researcher should avoid giving the impression that he can arrange for interviews in lesson times, as this might lead the pupil to identify the researcher as an authority figure with an official status within the school. For similar reasons the researcher takes care to establish the confidentiality of pupil interview data.

Whilst the researcher must avoid presenting himself as an authority figure to either teachers or pupils, he must also avoid behaving in a way which upsets the expectations which teachers and pupils have about appropriate adult behaviour. The researcher is not a member of staff, and neither is he a pupil. The researcher has to combine approachability and trustworthiness with the image of being of a status worthy of the subjects' time and effort.

How can the researcher deal with the possibility that subjects might present merely plausible, as opposed to authentic responses?

The present study is principally concerned with the actual thinking that underlies teachers' and pupils' classroom activity. It is necessary, therefore, to devise a strategy which helps researcher and informant to distinguish between responses which represent such thinking, and responses which are *post hoc* rationalizations of behaviour, or expressions of espoused rather than practised theory.

In order to deal with this problem a method of 'informant' style (Powney and Watts, 1987) interviewing has been adopted. The rationale of informant interviews is that the interviewer allows the shape and direction of the interview to be largely dictated by the unfolding pattern of the interviewee's perspective. In the present study, the interview method is designed to facilitate the interviewees' recall of particular and personal cognitive representation of the lessons being studied. This approach bears interesting associations with the technique of 'cognitive interviewing', in its adherence to the view that accurate recall is often an idiosyncratic process, involving the activation of cues which have no obvious relevance to anyone other than the subject (Roy, 1991). Subjects are initially encouraged to recall any good or successful aspect of the lesson which is prominent in their memories. These 'surface features' are then explored and developed through a process of elaboration, which is based on the researcher's use of prompts. The intention of this approach is to ensure that interviewees' accounts are grounded in the actual events of lessons. Where interviewees do make generalized remarks the researcher requests exemplification. It is, therefore, possible to distinguish between responses that are so grounded and those which are generalized. Similarly, responses relating to events that have been directly observed and recalled by the researcher can be considered to have a higher degree of reliability than those which relate to events not observed by the researcher.

In the final analysis it will be those items of interview data which are most thoroughly grounded in classroom events, and expounded with consistency and intricate detail that will form our most useful and interesting data.

Commonality

In the absence of spontaneous commonality of teacher and pupil perceptions of significant classroom events, how might it be possible for the researcher to engineer such commonality without influencing or interfering with the flow of subjects' spontaneous perceptions?

The problem here is, if pupils and teachers recall entirely different events from one another when talking about the same lessons, what basis will we have for exploring relationships between teachers' accounts of effective teaching processes and pupils' accounts of effective learning? To avoid the dangers of losing valuable data of this type a supplementary section is added to the interview procedure. Where there is little or no spontaneous commonality between teacher and pupil interviews, a more directive phase will be entered toward the end of interviews in which examples gleaned from teacher interviews will be presented to pupils for their comments, and vice versa. As far as possible such material will be introduced in non-leading terms, so as to avoid pre-empting the interviewee's response.

Use of this approach would allow us to discover similarities and differences between the ways in which teachers and pupils construe, explain and evaluate given events or aspects of lessons. However, a need to depend at all heavily on this approach would itself indicate an important finding: that salient teaching successes in teachers' eyes bear little relationship to salient learning successes in the eyes of their pupils. We hope therefore that our need for this approach will be limited.

Conclusion

In this chapter we have sought to explain the aspirations guiding our research project, some of the methodological issues which arise for us and some of our thinking about how these issues should be addressed. We hope that this discussion of a project at its planning stage will be of some interest; we are in no doubt about the importance of the issues. The quality and value of the research will of course depend not only on the good sense of our aspirations and of our methodological thinking but also on the discipline, the self-critical awareness and the reflexivity with which we conduct the research.

Acknowledgment

This project has been funded by the Economic and Social Research Council through its 'Initiative on Innovation and Change in Education: The Quality of Teaching and Learning'.

References

ANDERSON, L. (1981) 'Short term student responses to classroom instruction', *The Elementary School Journal*, **82**, 15, pp. 97–108.

BALL, S. and BOWE, R. (1990) 'Subject to Change? Subject departments and the implementation of National Curriculum Policy: An overview of the issues', unpublished paper, *Centre for Educational Studies*, King's College, London.

BIGGS, J. (1987) *Student Approaches to Learning and Studying*, Melbourne, Australian Council for Educational Research.

BROWN, S. and McINTYRE, D. (1982) 'Costs and rewards of innovation: Taking account of the teachers' viewpoint', in OLSON, J. (Ed.) *Innovation in the Science Curriculum*, London, Croom Helm.

BROWN, S. and McINTYRE, D. (1992) *Making Sense of Teaching*, Buckingham, Open University Press.

CLARK, C. (1986) 'Ten years of conceptual development in research on teacher thinking', in BEN-PERETZ, M., BROMME, R. and HALKES, R. (Eds.) *Advances of Research on Teacher Thinking*, Lisse, Swets Zeitlinger.

DESFORGES, C. and MCNAMARA, D. (1977) 'One man's heuristic is another man's blindfold: Some comments on applying social science to educational practice', *British Journal of Teacher Education*, **3**, 1, pp. 27–39.

DESFORGES, C. and MCNAMARA, D. (1979) 'Theory and practice: Methodological procedures for the objectification of craft knowledge', *British Journal of Teacher Education*, **5**, 2, pp. 145–52.

DOYLE, W. (1977) 'Learning the classroom environment: An ecological analysis', *Journal of Teacher Education*, **28**, 6, pp. 51–5.

HARGREAVES, D., HESTER, S. and MELLOR, F. (1975) *Deviance in Classrooms*, London, Routledge and Kegan Paul.

HOUSE, E. and LAPAN, S.D. (1989) 'Teacher appraisal', in SIMONS, H. and ELLIOTT, J. (Eds.) *Rethinking Appraisal and Assessment*, Buckingham, Open University Press.

JOHNSTON, K. (1988) 'Changing teachers' conceptions of teaching and learning', in CALDERHEAD, J. (Ed.) *Teachers' Professional Learning*, Lewes, Falmer Press.

LEINHARDT, G. (1988) 'Situated knowledge and expertise in teaching', in CALDERHEAD, J. (Ed.) *Teachers' Professional Learning*, Lewes, Falmer Press.

MCNAMARA, D. and DESFORGES, C. (1978) 'The social sciences, teacher education and the objectification of craft knowledge', *British Journal of Teacher Education*, **4**, 1, pp. 17–36.

OLSON, J. (1984) 'What makes teachers tick? Considering the routines of teaching', in HALKES, R. and OLSON, J. (Eds.) *Teacher Thinking*, Lisse, Swets Zeitlinger.

PETERSON, P. and SWING, P. (1982) 'Beyond time on task: Students' reports of their thought processes during classroom instruction', *The Elementary School Journal*, **82**, 15, pp. 481–91.

POWNEY, J. and WATTS, M. (1987) *Interviewing in Educational Research*, London, Routledge and Kegan Paul.

ROY, D. (1991) 'Improving recall by eyewitnesses through the cognitive interview', *The Psychologist*, **14**, 9, pp. 398–400.

SHULMAN, L. (1986) 'Paradigms and research programmes in the study of teaching: A comparative perspective', in WITTROCK, M.C. (Ed.) *Handbook of Research on Teaching*, Third Edition, New York, Macmillan.

TOM, A. (1984) *Teaching as a Moral Craft*, New York, Longman.

WANG, M. (1990) *Special Education: Research and Practice*, Oxford, Pergamon.

WANG, M.C. and WALBERG, H.J. (1983) 'Evaluating educational programmes', *Educational Evaluation and Policy Analysis*, 5, pp. 347–66.

WEINSTEIN, C.F. and MAYER, R.R. (1986) 'The teaching of learning strategies', in WITTROCK, M.C. (Ed.) *Handbook of Research on Teaching*, Third Edition, New York, Macmillan.

WINNE, P. and MARX, R. (1982) 'Students' and teachers' views of thinking processes for classroom learning', *The Elementary School Journal*, **82**, 15, pp. 493–518.

WITTROCK, M. (1986) 'Students' thought processes', in WITTROCK, M. (Ed.) *Handbook of Research on Teaching*, Third Edition, New York, Macmillan.

WOODS, P. (1990) *The Happiest Days? How Pupils Cope with School*, Basingstoke, Falmer Press.

2   Process Product Research Revisited

Philip Adey

Almost all reports of academic research conclude that 'more research is needed'. Reports on the evaluation of INSET are different. They *start* with the observation that 'more research is needed'. For one who has come relatively recently to the investigation of what might count as effective INSET, it is surprising to discover (a) how little is known about the effect of particular procedures on particular outcomes and (b) how often this observation is made.

Daresh (1987), reviewing research on staff development and INSET reported in over 400 journal articles and over 500 doctoral dissertations found not one use of 'true experimental design which would have permitted the researcher to manipulate variables of interest' (p. 5). The most popular data collection method was the questionnaire, followed by observations, interviews and document analysis. He does not mention pupils' learning.

Of the studies which looked at the effects of INSET on teachers or educational administrators, (some 15 per cent of the whole), '. . . perhaps the only generalized finding that came from the review of these studies was that staff development or in-service education tended to have little or no discernable effect on the attitudes or observable behaviours of educators . . .' (let alone on pupils) (p. x).

Bolam (1987) spells out some methodological problems which he sees as at least partially responsible for the paucity of evidence on the effect of INSET on teacher behaviour or on pupil learning. I suspect that under closer scrutiny many of the reasons he proposes will prove to be unconvincing, but that is not my purpose here.

So, what are the difficulties of evaluating an INSET programme in terms of whether or not it has had any measurable effect on pupils? Here are some of them:

- **Interaction effects.** Nearly twenty years ago Gardner (1974) presented an elegant study showing how the use made by different pupils of a given teacher behaviour was mediated by personality, such that the application of a simple process-product model could easily lead to erroneous conclusions. Where a particular teacher characteristic at first sight appeared unrelated to pupil performance, deeper analysis showed that it positively affected pupils of one personality type, and negatively affected pupils of a different personality type.

- **The dilution effect.** A teacher, like anyone else, is subjected to a great variety of stimuli every day. An INSET event, however impactful it may appear to be, has to compete with all of the other stimuli in shaping the teacher's behaviour. The ascription of a particular behaviour to a particular INSET experience is not necessarily straightforward. Exactly the same is true of the pupils' experiences. It is difficult to ascribe a particular pupil outcome to a particular stimulus provided by the teacher. Multiply these effects together, and the link between an INSET ir.put and a pupil outcome becomes very tenuous indeed.

- **Non-uniformity of input.** Eraut *et al.* (1988) explain that it was not feasible to look for pupil effects in the local evaluation of TRIST, since the TRIST input was of such a various nature that it would not have been meaningful to look for specific changes in pupils' learning or attitudes. I suppose that one could pursue the issue of what TRIST inputs did have in common, that may possibly have been related to pupil learning, but I doubt if such a line of investigation would be profitable.

- **Uncertainty over best possible effect of an input.** So much of what we do in INSET courses is based on unsupported assumptions about what constitutes effective teaching and learning. 'Process skills' in science, 'the communicative method' in language teaching, and 'new mathematics' have all had their dawns and middays of fashion amongst practitioners and teacher educators. The measurability of outcomes associated with such assumed good practice remains problematical. The problem is that if you are not sure whether or not teaching system X works, in any sense, then an evaluation of INSET in system X which shows no gain in pupil learning may either be because the INSET was poorly delivered, or because system X does not work. There is no way of telling which.

From this brief list of difficulties, we can draw up criteria for possible types of INSET for which process-product evaluation might be useful. Let us consider each in turn, and see how they might be overcome. I will start with the last, since this where I think we have a new advantage.

Uncertainty

Over the last ten years we have developed, trialled, and validated a method of teaching and learning which has been shown to lead to long-term gains in secondary students' ability to learn (Adey and Shayer, 1990; Shayer and Adey, 1992a; Shayer and Adey, 1992b; Shayer and Adey, 1993). This was the Cognitive Acceleration through Science Education (CASE) project, on which I do not plan to comment, other than to summarize the INSET provided to the project teachers. This consisted of six days over two years, made up of four single days' attendance at college, and one residential weekend in the country, plus visits once or twice per term to the teachers in their schools. These were not simply observation or evaluation visits, but opportunities to participate in CASE lessons with the teachers, to some extent to model the sort of techniques we thought would be helpful, and to discuss the lesson afterwards in some detail. (This model of INSET actually follows the prescription of Joyce and Showers (1988) that no staff development programme is effective if it does not include an element of coaching the teachers in their own school environment, although at the time we did not realize that this was what we were doing).

Having established that we do have a system that has been shown to work under the conditions of its development, we can now address the 'uncertainty' problem with more certainty. If we run INSET programmes to introduce the CASE method (see Adey, Shayer and Yates, 1989) to a new group of teachers, and there is no effect on their pupils, then we can be fairly certain that the INSET job has not been good enough. Knowing that CASE teaching (our system X), when thoroughly taken on board by teachers, does have an effect on pupil learning allows us to isolate the INSET as the weak link if we do not get a similar result after a new and modified programme of training.

Non-uniformity

Well, there is not much one can say about this. To state the problem is to state its remedy: make sure that if you are evaluating INSET, the INSET has fairly clear aims in terms of both learning outcomes and of the methodology which is intended to produce them. I am not talking here of anything so restricting as behavioural objectives, but considerably more than pious aims to 'improve practice' are required.

Dilution

I have a gin-and-tonic model here. Both gin and tonic have fairly distinctive flavours. If you cannot taste the gin (or cannot detect it by the effect that it has on you) then you need to increase the concentration. It is unrealistic to think that a one day INSET session is going to have much lasting effect on teachers' practice. On the other hand Joyce and Showers' (1988) prescription that a teacher must practice a new technique at least thirty times before it becomes an automated part of their repertoire strikes me as overkill. It becomes a matter of empirical investigation to discover the minimum concentration which does produce a permanent effect, for whatever effect is desired, given some potential certainty of the effect and clarity of objectives dealt with above.

Interaction

Interaction remains a problem. In the CASE project we did find that amongst each group of pupils, some (between 20 per cent and 40 per cent) achieved gains of two standard deviations or more, while the remainder showed no difference from controls. Whilst this allowed us to report overall significant gains, it left us wondering what were the pupil characteristics of the high-gain group that differentiated them from the no-gain group. Since we had used no personality or learning-style measurements, we have no way of answering this. This story is salutary, and emphasizes the value of some sort of personality inventory even in relatively hard-nosed process-product research designs ostensibly looking only for cognitive gains.

What next?

Given the availability of a tested system within our field of cognitive acceleration, we are now in a stronger position to establish experimental designs to investigate some interesting variables in INSET. For example, what is the relative effect of different types of school-focused work in an INSET programme? Both INSET folk wisdom and common sense suggest that there will be a greater and longer lasting effect on teachers' practice if the programme includes the trainer working with teachers in their own schools. But such work is expensive. I believe now that it would be feasible to provide INSET programmes to, say, two groups of teachers such that both groups received the same total hours of training, but group A's was all college based, and group B's was a mixture of college and school-based. Pre- to post-test gains of pupils learning would tell whether the extra cost of group B's treatment was justified. It might well show that group A's programme, although cheaper, was a complete waste of money if it had no effect on student's learning.

Joyce (personal communication) claims that much of the effect of tutors' work in schools can be achieved by teachers coaching each other. Again this is a claim that requires verification, and I do not have to spell out a simple research design by which light could be thrown on it, nor any of many subtle complexities that might be added to that design, given the research funding.

One more example: just how important is it that teachers understand the psychological basis of a teaching method for them to deliver it effectively? In the case of CASE, it might be argued that without a good understanding of the nature of formal operational thinking, a teacher will not be able to respond flexibly and intelligently to the day-to-day instances where she has an opportunity to encourage such thinking. On the other hand, some might claim that delivery of the method is a high level skill which can be learnt, as one learns to drive a car well, without much understanding of why what one does works. Although more difficult to operationalize than the school-based/college-based question, I believe that this also is an old question which we are now in a better position to address through quantitative research designs.

Obtaining funding for such research is another matter. So far I have not been successful, partly no doubt because my project proposals have not been adequately structured, but also perhaps for two reasons which could affect us all: (i) In days when central government funded a lot of INSET, one might have been able to sell such research in terms of whether they were getting value for money. With INSET funding devolved to authority and school level, no individual unit has sufficient funds to address research questions which are not specifically related to their own programmes. (ii) A research project which has the potential of showing that much of the INSET we have profitably been engaged in for years was a complete waste of money could be rather embarrassing. Maybe it would be more peaceful to continue to muddle along, selling INSET to schools and 'evaluating' it by asking the participants how they feel. Who wants to derail the gravy train?

References

ADEY, P.S., SHAYER, M. and YATES, C. (1989) *Thinking Science: The Curriculum Materials of the CASE Project*, Basingstoke, Macmillan Education.

ADEY, P.S. and SHAYER, M. (1990) 'Accelerating the development of formal thinking in middle and high school students', *Journal of Research in Science Teaching*, **27**, 3, pp. 267–85.

BOLAM, R. (1987) 'What is effective INSET?' in *Professional Development and INSET*, Slough, NFER.

DARESH, J.C. (1987) 'Research trends in staff development and inservice education', *Journal of Education for Teaching*, **13**, 1, pp. 3–11.

ERAUT, M., PENNYCUICK, D. and RADNOR, H. (1988) *Local Evaluation of INSET: A meta-evaluation of TRIST Evaluations*, Bristol, National Development Centre for School Management.

GARDNER, P.L. (1974) 'Research on teacher effects: Critique of a traditional paradigm', *British Journal of Educational Psychology*, **44**, 2, pp. 123–30.

JOYCE, B. and SHOWERS, B. (1988) *Student Achievement through Staff Development*, New York, Longman.

SHAYER, M. and ADEY, P. (1992a) 'Accelerating the development of formal thinking in middle and high school students II: Post-project effects on science achievement', *Journal of Research in Science Teaching*, **29**, 1, pp. 81–92.

SHAYER, M. and ADEY, P.S. (1992b) 'Accelerating the developing of formal operational thinking in high school pupils. III: Post-project effects on public examinations in science and mathematics', *Journal of Research in Science Teaching*, **29**, 10, pp. 1101–1115.

SHAYER, M. and ADEY, P.S. (1993) 'Accelerating the development of formal operational thinking in high school pupils, IV: Three years on after a two year intervention', *Journal of Research in Science Teaching*, **130**, 4, pp. 351–366.

3   Changing Classroom Practice Through INSET: Towards a Holistic Model

Kay Kinder and John Harland

Introduction

In the UK, in theory at least, the most organized and highly funded method of attempting to bring about improvements and changes in classroom practice is through the in-service education and training of teachers (IN-SET). Although INSET manifests itself in many different forms (e.g. statutory Professional Development Days in schools, higher degree courses in institutions of higher education, school and classroom-based support from LEA advisory teachers, residential weekends, professional development action-research groups and networks), the ultimate, if not always explicit, justification for most INSET activity is that it will contribute to the process of making classroom practice more effective. Given the substantial professional and political pressure for improvements in teaching and learning, in-service provision, as a key mediation vehicle, assumes the onerous responsibility of promising to facilitate such changes and developments in classroom practice. Looked at from this perspective, it is clearly vital to take up the central theme explored in this book and ask to what extent can and does INSET fulfil this promise? Under what conditions does INSET precipitate changes in classroom practice? Alternatively, why and how does INSET as a mediation process break down so that little impact on classroom practice is achieved? In this chapter, we draw on the results of a case study research project which addressed these questions, and outline a new holistic typology of INSET outcomes as a device for discussing the complex mediation between INSET and changes in classroom practice. For a more detailed exposition of the model, the research and the in-service scheme on which it was based, the reader could consult Kinder and Harland (1991) and Kinder *et al.* (1991).

Earlier studies

Throughout the 1970s and early 1980s, the focus of most research into INSET corroborated Henderson's (1978) criticism that empirical studies tended to concentrate on delivery processes and the experience of in-service provision rather than their effects. In the last five years, more re-searchers have responded to this imbalance and, as a result, a growing number of studies which contain or accentuate analyses of the effects of INSET have appeared (e.g. Dienye, 1987; Evans and Hopkins, 1988; Halpin *et al.*, 1990; Kinder *et al.*, 1991; Vulliamy and Webb, 1991; Cope *et al.*, 1992; Harland and Kinder, 1992). A number of tendencies are apparent in these studies: (i) they tend to examine the effects of higher degree courses, (ii) the researchers are often based in the same institution as the course providers, (iii) questionnaires or one-off interviews are the main data source, and (iv) they tend to rely on teacher self-report data which are not cor-roborated against other sources or perspectives. By way of contrast, the research (Kinder and Harland, 1991) upon which this present chapter is based, afforded an opportunity to complement and extend the above studies by (i) examining the processes and outcomes of an LEA advisory teacher team providing school- and classroom-based INSET as opposed to an accredited course, (ii) the researchers were independent in that they were not part of an institution providing INSET, (iii) longitudinal case studies with repeated interviews over three years were the main data source, and (iv) teachers' self-reports of the effects of the INSET provision were cross-checked against classroom observational data and interviews with pupils. On the basis of this research, we would argue that this last point deserves particular attention when devising appropriate methodologies for re-searching changes in classroom practice as a result of INSET involvement or professional development programmes. In some cases, for example, pupil accounts and observational material contradicted teachers' claims about changed practice; in many other cases, it appeared that the series of classroom observations ensured a greater validity and grounded reality to teachers' accounts of the degree of changes to their practice.

In designing the project, the most influential research was the work of the American writers, Joyce and Showers. Two dimensions of their work were especially pertinent. First, their emphasis on the value of offering teachers support and 'transfer skills' at the point of any new teaching and learning implementations in the classroom (Joyce and Showers, 1982) resonated with the experiences of many of the teachers we studied. Sec-ond, and more significantly, for present purposes, their model of INSET outcomes or the effects of INSET directed at changing teacher behaviour in the classroom (Joyce and Showers, 1980) proved inadequate as a con-ceptual framework for making sense of the effects observed and reported in our study.

As part of a matrix between forms of training and level of impact, Joyce and Showers (1980) describe training outcomes under four categories:

- general awareness of new skills;
- organized knowledge of underlying concepts and theory;

- learning of new skills;
- application on-the-job.

Our original intention was to apply this typology of outcomes to chart the effects of the in-service training we were studying. However, analysis of the effects of the INSET scheme suggested that the nature and range of outcomes were more complex and broad-ranging than those contained in the model advanced by Joyce and Showers. Furthermore, the outcomes evident in our data, but omitted in the American researchers' typology, appeared to have significant consequences for any analysis of the relationship between INSET inputs, and impacts on teachers' classroom practice. Thus, while Joyce and Showers' notions of 'awareness', 'knowledge and skills' and 'application on-the-job' are readily taken on board as important and empirically sustained outcomes, the typology derived from our evidence is more extensive. As an example of the extensions to the model, it should be noted that Joyce and Showers' typology implies that the challenge of in-service training is principally concerned with capability and cognitive outcomes. Evidence from our research suggests that there are four other factors which have been totally omitted from the classification summarized above. Motivation and value orientation changes are not considered by Joyce and Showers, yet our study suggests these can be highly significant outcomes, which can have a crucial influence on teachers' subsequent practices in the classroom.

Before describing the model desired from this research, some brief details of the study and its methods are necessary.

Outline of the research project

The research was commissioned by Calderdale LEA. It formed a three year study (Kinder and Harland, 1991) into the longer-term effects of an Education Support Grant (ESG) scheme in Primary Science and Technology. This involved looking at the science practice under way in five primary schools following the scheme's school-based input from advisory teachers, its provision of £200 for equipment and materials, and the contracted appointment of a school science co-ordinator. The research used case study methods, including a series of return visits to interview headteachers, science co-ordinators, teachers, pupils, advisory teachers and LEA advisers, as well as classroom observations of advisory teachers working alongside client teachers and of subsequent science activities taught by the teachers involved. The researchers also observed two related residential courses. The study took place between 1988 and 1990, and therefore covered practice both before and during National Curriculum implementation. Although the research focus was in one sector of education and one curriculum area, drawing out any general implications for INSET planning and provision was always intended by the sponsor.

One of the requests from the Calderdale sponsor was to provide a general model of INSET outcomes which would specifically aid planning. The researchers analyzed all the data for evidence of the effects of INSET on classroom practice, noting both positive and negative effects, and those which the providers had intended as well as those which they had not. A composite list of some forty-four different kinds of statements on impact was yielded by the data which was then reduced to nine broad categories. These nine different categories of INSET outcomes became the constituents of a typology. It should be stressed that the typology reflects the intended aim of the in-service scheme studied, namely changes in classroom practice. The typology may have taken a different shape if career development or management skills had been the main aims.

A typology of INSET outcomes

The nine INSET outcomes which made up the typology are summarized below.

1. Material and provisionary outcomes are the physical resources which result from participation in INSET activities (e.g. worksheets, equipment, handbooks). The research indicates such outcomes can have a positive and substantial influence on teachers' classroom practice. However, it suggests that ensuring an impact on practice usually requires other intermediary outcomes such as *motivation* and new *knowledge and skills.*

2. Informational outcomes are defined as 'the state of being briefed or cognizant of background facts and news about curriculum and management developments, including their implications for practice'. It is distinct from new *knowledge and skills* which is intended to imply more critical and deeper understanding. The research raises the issue of the timing and neutrality of any INSET delivering informational outcomes, as well as its likely minimal impact on classroom practice.

3. New awareness (a term used often by teachers themselves) is defined as a perceptual shift from previous assumptions of what constitutes the appropriate content and delivery of a particular curriculum area. For example, as a result of the ESG scheme, a teacher reported being aware that science is not about 'chemical formulae and test tubes but about children investigating'. However, the research corroborates teachers' own assertions that changed awareness is no guarantee of changed practice. It generally required the presence of the fourth outcome — defined as *value congruence.*

4. Value congruence outcomes refer to the personalized versions of curriculum and classroom management which inform a

practitioner's teaching, and how far these 'individual codes of practice' come to coincide with INSET messages about 'good practice'. Thus, for example, teachers may be made aware of investigative group learning for science by listening to and seeing the advisory teachers at work, but whereas some might adopt the practice wholeheartedly, others might still prefer whole-class delivery as the approach they remain comfortable with. Value congruence with the INSET message became a crucial factor in influencing the extent of subsequent classroom implementation.

5 Affective outcomes acknowledge there is an emotional experience inherent in any learning situation. The research revealed some examples of negative affective outcomes (e.g. teachers who felt demoralized by the INSET experience). It was found that initial positive affective outcomes could sometimes be short-lived without a sense of accompanying enhanced expertise. Nevertheless, such outcomes may be a useful, and even necessary, precursor for changing practice.

6 Motivational and attitudinal outcomes refer to enhanced enthusiasm and motivation to implement the ideas received during INSET experiences. For instance, a teacher may claim to feel 'inspired' by observing an advisory teacher's way of working and attempt to emulate it. Like affective outcomes, these attitudinal outcomes function as a particularly important pre-condition to developments in practice, but can also be short-lived or superficial if other outcomes — such as provisionary or new knowledge and skills — are not present. This point is especially pertinent to the 'mandated motivation' often underpinning the implementation of new National Curriculum subjects. However, like affective outcomes they may function as particularly important precursors in impacting on practice.

7 Knowledge and skills denotes deeper levels of understanding, critical reflexivity and theoretical rationales, with regard to both curriculum content (e.g. enhanced understanding of scientific concepts) and teaching/learning processes (e.g. the management of investigations).

8 Institutional outcomes acknowledge that INSET can have an important collective impact on groups of teachers and their practice. The value of consensus, collaboration and mutual support when attempting curriculum innovation in the classroom is fairly obvious: school-based INSET or the work of school curriculum leaders was often targeted at achieving institutional outcomes.

9 Impact on practice recognizes the ultimate intention to bring about changes in practice, either directly (e.g. by supporting the transfer of new skills to the teacher's repertoire in the classroom) or though the indirect route of other outcomes mentioned above.

A tentative hierarchy of outcomes

When teachers' accounts of the impact of the INSET experience on their classroom repertoire were juxtaposed with classroom observation of the teachers' science practice, it was apparent that the presence of certain outcomes was more likely to achieve developments in practice than others. Hence, a tentative sequence of hierarchy of outcomes was developed. Assuming that influencing classroom practice is the intended INSET goal, the following exploratory 'ordering of outcomes' was proposed:

INSET
3rd Order   PROVISIONARY : INFORMATION : NEW AWARENESS
2nd Order   MOTIVATION : AFFECTIVE : INSTITUTIONAL
1st Order   VALUE CONGRUENCE : KNOWLEDGE & SKILLS
IMPACT ON PRACTICE

The evidence of the evaluation suggests that INSET experiences which focus on (or are perceived as offering) only third order outcomes are least likely to impact on practice, unless other higher order outcomes are also achieved or already exist. The interdependency or knock-on effect of some outcomes was evident (e.g. provisionary outcomes could be highly motivating; or a teacher who has been enthused by the INSET experience might seek out further courses to increase her knowledge and skills). However, it was the presence of the first order INSET outcomes which consistently coincided with a substantial impact on practice, although these in turn might well require the presence of other lower order outcomes — such as provisionary or institutional — to ensure sustained implementation. Our tentative conclusion is that in order for INSET and related support mechanisms to mediate a change in classroom practice, all nine 'outcomes' (prioritized in the order suggested above) need to be present as pre-existing conditions or be achieved by the INSET activities.

Individual outcome routes

Teachers' accounts of the impact of the ESG scheme on their practice made clear that the in-service activities had had a very varied influence: different teachers in effect nominated different outcomes accruing from the same INSET provision. For instance, some stated they were highly motivated to incorporate science in their classroom repertoire after the ESG in-service, while others were far less enthusiastic, conceding only that new equipment had been made available or that they had received information and new insights into the LEA's policy on science practice. These differences suggested that INSET consumers have a unique 'outcome route' following an in-service experience and rarely achieve exactly the same permutation of outcomes as another colleague. When individual outcome-routes were matched to subsequent teaching, the typology outlined above proved helpful in analyzing the reasons underpinning the effect on the classroom practice of individual teachers. To illustrate this use of the model, two such outcome routes are reproduced below from Kinder and Harland (1991). (It should be noted that if a teacher's description of the ESG scheme's impact did not include a particular outcome, it is omitted from the diagram of their outcome-route.)

Teacher One

Practice:

Teacher One referred to a continuing preference for formal teaching approaches, and the pre-eminence of 'the basics' in the curriculum offered to children. She indicated openly that the scheme had minimal impact on her classroom work — very little science was done before, and only a little more after the scheme. Any science activity was usually undertaken as a whole-class teacher-led discussion. Classroom observation corroborated the teacher's continuing unfamiliarity with investigative, group learning.

Outcome-route: Teacher One

3rd Order	Provisionary:	: New awareness
2nd Order	:	: (Institutional)
1st Order	:	

These third order outcomes were the limit of the positive outcomes referred to by Teacher One. No positive second order outcomes were mentioned (although the after school INSET was enjoyed): the teacher claimed to remain 'unhappy' about teaching science and was made conscious of the enormous gulf between the advisory teacher's practice and values and her own. However, the co-ordinator was said to provide resources and 'chivvy along', hence a possible institutional outcome.

Thus, Teacher One's outcome-route broke down at the lowest level and evidence of impact on practice was negligible.

Teacher Two

Practice:

Teacher Two expressed a strong sense of the looming national imperative to deliver science in the primary curriculum. She was particularly concerned about her continuing lack of scientific knowledge, and made extensive use of the teacher materials and workcards provided by the £200. She acknowledged that she may have 'picked up a way of questioning children in science' from the advisory teachers, but found their notion of facilitating children's problem-solving inconsistent with her own limited knowledge and confidence. Within an efficient classroom management strategy that ensured she could invest a good deal of time with her science groups, she offered investigative scientific activities based on commercial workcards. However, the concepts appeared to have been rather too sophisticated for the age-group — and, by her own admission — to some extent the teacher herself!

Outcome-route: Teacher Two

3rd Order	Provisionary:	Information:	New awareness
2nd Order	Motivation:	Affective :	Institutional
1st Order		:	

This teacher had an altogether more complex and positive response to the scheme. All third order outcomes were referred to: availability of teacher materials; insights and information on the 'LEA policy' for primary science and the reassurance of the message that her Environmental Studies work already contained a good deal of science. In turn, these third order outcomes were said to have activated second order outcomes which, though initially very positive, were also acknowledged to be relatively short term. Ultimately, the National Curriculum imperative maintained motivation to undertake science, as well as support from the co-ordinator. Lack of scientific knowledge was seen as the major stumbling block to a genuine valuation of science in this teacher's curriculum; a conscientious tokenism was the admitted result.

Using the model to evaluate the effects of INSET

Developing the analytical application of the model, the researchers used it as an evaluation tool in a study commissioned by Kirklees LEA (Kinder *et al.*, 1991); focusing on the impact of school-based INSET on classroom practice. Part of the data-collection involved explaining the typology and its language to a sample of twelve teachers and four heads/school INSET co-ordinators. Each was then asked to analyze their different INSET experiences using the nine outcomes descriptors. In this way, the teachers were being asked to make their own audit of the effects of INSET.

By undertaking this outcome-audit, the teachers were able to explain with precision and economy why certain INSET experiences did little for their practice, while other in-service had considerable impact. In other words, the typology became an aid to defining which INSET was counting and which was not. Equally, the teachers' audits were able to pinpoint how the impact of some INSET could have been greater if other outcomes had occurred. Two contrasting examples are reproduced below:

INSET INPUT:

Principles and Practice of Nursery Education

3rd order

Provisionary	**Information**	**New Awareness**
printed booklet of all we covered, names and addresses, resource materials	first learnt about workshop approach: shown slides and philosophy behind it	heightened my awareness of potential and possibilities

2nd order

Motivation	**Affective**	**Institutional**
inspired me to look more closely at my nursery provision and make it the best I could. Placed more value on nursery education. I wanted to go on the nursery leadership course as a result	exciting and stimulating really enjoyed it all	tried to heighten profile of the nursery in the life of the school

1st order

Value Congruence

very much in tune with organizers and those who gave input. Slight incongruence with workshop approach, but this was not imposed, we were free to evaluate and take out what was relevant and useful to us.

Knowledge and Skills

deeper knowledge of importance of nursery's physical structures in meeting children's needs, new skills, e.g. drawing up and producing criteria for profiles: new ways of presenting stories

Impact on Practice

introduced recording of child observations

Comment

This primary teacher's thorough encounter with a serial course in nursery education practice and principles was augmented by visits to nurseries locally and beyond, sometimes undertaken during Professional Development Days. It stands as a testament to possible impact when time, commitment and a comprehensive in-service provision are given to further a clearly defined specialist interest and professional need. The sense of not just professional development, but what might be termed professional self-realization, comes through in her outcome-audit, as all three orders to outcome are acknowledged. It is also worth noting that the audit suggests a direct translation of acquired knowledge into practice (i.e. the observation and profiling system). Yet, what also has clearly resulted from the INSET is a confident, expert and (as one secondary teacher described himself) *'empowered'* professional.

The second example of a primary teacher's outcome-audit describes the impact of a short course.

INSET INPUT

Maths Assessment INSET

3rd order   :   :

2nd order   :   :
(Motivation)
[yes]

1st order
   Value Congruence:
   started me thinking about
   problem solving, I'm going to
   start using a TV programme . . .

Impact on Practice
   . . . I'm going to start this term with the top group first

Comment

Here a teacher is apparently motivated by a one-day course which she claims gave her some 'ideological' commitment to initiating a particular teaching and learning approach. However, the apparent absence of provisionary and new knowledge and skills outcomes means she delays and then makes only a tentative start — relying on a TV programme and electing to begin by giving only her more able children the opportunity to work in this way. Perhaps this well illustrates the limitations of short one-off courses, at the same time demonstrating the value of being motivated by and 'congruent with' what was reputed to be a particularly impressive course. The first order value congruence outcome appears to have ensured a continuing commitment despite an apparent lack of materials or resources necessary for instant implementation. However, the lack of provisionary outcomes may be a significant omission: indeed, in another example of outcome-audits, one teacher identified motivational and new knowledge and skills outcomes from a day's maths course on 'multilink', but stated categorically that there had been no impact on practice because there was no such equipment in school.

One further use for the typology has also been suggested. Both school and LEA INSET managers have indicated that, as well as providing a structure for reflecting on what the INSET actually does for teachers' practice, the outcomes model may also serve as a way of analyzing more precisely what kinds of INSET outcomes should be achieved in order to best meet an individual practitioner's (or school's) particular professional development needs. Thus, the model is no longer only a post-course evaluation instrument but one that could be used in pre-course diagnosis and discussion of particular training requirements.

Conclusion

Using data generated through two studies of INSET provision, a typology of the outcomes of INSET directed at changing teachers' classroom practice has been proposed. Our evidence points to the conclusion that change in classroom practice requires the nine 'outcomes' to exist as prior conditions or to be attained through a sequence of INSET activities and associated support mechanisms. Accordingly, it is felt that the model can contribute to our understanding of the effects of INSET and inform practice by providing a useful tool for:

- evaluating the outcomes of INSET, especially on classroom practice;
- diagnosing individual professional developmental needs; and
- planning a sustained and co-ordinated sequence of in-service activities and support in order to meet specific outcomes.

References

Cope, P., Inglis, B., Riddell, S. and Sulhunt, O. (1992) 'The Value of In-service Degrees: Teachers' perceptions of their impact', *British Education Research Journal*, **18**, 3.

Dienye, N.E. (1987) 'The effect of inservice education', *British Journal of Inservice Education*, **14**, 1, pp. 48–51.

Evans, M. and Hopkins, D. (1988) 'School climate and the psychological state of the individual teacher as factors affecting the utilisation of educational ideas', following an in-service.

Halpin, D., Croll, P. and Redman, K. (1990) 'Teachers' Perceptions of the Effects of In-Service Education', *British Education Research Journal*, **16**, 2.

Harland, J. and Kinder, K. (1992) *Mathematics and Science Courses for Primary Teachers: Lessons for the Future*, Slough, NFER/DES.

Henderson, E.S. (1978) *The Evaluation of In-Service Teacher Training*, Beckenham, Croom Helm.

Joyce, B. and Showers, B. (1980) 'Improving in-service training: The messages of research', *Educational Leadership*, Feb. pp. 379–85.

Joyce, B. and Showers, B. (1982) 'The Coaching of Teaching', *Educational Leadership*, October, pp. 379–85.

Joyce, B. and Showers, B. (1988) *Student Achievement Through Staff Development*, London, Longham.

Kinder, K. and Harland, J. (1991) *The Impact of INSET: The Case of Primary Science*, Slough, NFER.

Kinder, K., Harland, J. and Wooten, M. (1991) *The Impact of School-focused INSET on Classroom Practice*, Slough, NFER.

Vulliamy, G. and Webb, R. (1991) 'Teacher Research and Educational Change: An empirical study', *British Education Research Journal*, **17**, N3, pp. 219–36.

Part 2

Intended Change and Observed Outcomes

Part 2   Intended Change and Observed Outcomes

The process and purpose of change is constructed in the context of general and specific conditions. In education it is those general factors, the National Curriculum, Local Management of Schools, and so on, which determine the background to institutional change. Nevertheless it is also apparent that within this framework, which is ideological as well as bureaucratic, there is a relative autonomy that allows for differences in how policy is implemented.

This section allows us to consider three different examinations of intervention to bring about change; a secondary subject curriculum project, external local authority intervention to influence classroom development, and the influence of the National Curriculum in influencing science curriculum provision in the primary school.

The demise of The Schools Council at the beginning of the 1980s, has been described as a significant indicator of a move from consideration of process to that of content as the major concern of curriculum change. The emphasis of the National Curriculum on prescribed knowledge and its implementation within a power coercive model is contrasted by Dalton with the 'reasoned persuasion' of former times. Dalton reviews this overly simplistic notion and contrasts it with the reality of two case studies of schools involved in a Schools Council project. The value of this analysis is shown by the findings of the study of primary science teaching, presented by Farrow. This indicates that following the designation, and elevation in status, of science as a core National Curriculum subject, factors at school level mediate against the intended change being achieved in practice. Farrow observes that '. . . . scope exists for a serious mismatch between expectations in terms of statutory requirements, and outcomes in terms of assessed ability, ...'. Reproduction of government intentions is hindered by the same sort of issues which affected the Geography for the Young School Leaver (GYSL) project. Dalton finds himself agreeing with Rudduck in the ability of schools to '. . . absorb and expel innovations that are at odds with the dominant structures and values that hold habit in place.' (Rudduck, 1986).

It is possible that the context of change is the predominant factor in its implementation. Many supporters of primary science welcomed the National Curriculum as it gave their area an enhanced role. The GYSL project had a similar rationality about its introduction, although both the approach to teaching and learning and the way in which it was introduced was very different to the statutory requirement of the National Curriculum. Perhaps they should both be seen as diverse examples of the attempt to establish an orthodoxy whether by process or content. In either case assumptions about delivery do not appear sufficiently to take into account the interference of school and teacher.

Chatwin, McGowan, Turner and Wick question the ability of schools to successfully support their own change, while deriding simplistic views of a 'systematic' approach to school improvement. As with the other two chapters in this section, they question the correspondence of classroom practice to the will of decision makers at other levels in the system. The current moves to limit the ability of local education authorities to intervene in schools, the responsibility for improvement to be placed on governing bodies and school management, is regarded as flawed. Senior school managers are found wanting in their ability to identify problems, engage as effective staff tutors and link school development objectives with classroom practice. The relative autonomy of departments and individual teachers is shown, in a similar fashion to the evidence of the two other chapters in this section, to deform the change intentions.

This section provides a reminder of the complexities of the translation of policy intention into practice.

Reference

RUDDUCK, J. (1986) *Understanding Curriculum*, Change Division of Education, University of Sheffield.

4   Common Curriculum but Diverse Experience

Tom Dalton

Knowledge and innovation

The observation of pupils working on the same curriculum programme in schools revealed major differences in the learning experience of the pupils, both between the schools and between classrooms in the same school. The programme being followed emanated from the Schools Council, Geography for the Young School Leaver (GYSL) project. The Schools Council style of operation might superficially seem to have little in common with the present workings of the DFE or the National Curriculum Council, the Schools Council exemplifying a model 'depending on reasoned persuasion, impartial analysis or reasoned argument and operating within a collegial framework — the former depending for its adoption on the force of statute — a power coercive model' (Becher, 1989).

Yet, on reflection, the way that a common Schools Council Programme was received, interpreted and implemented in different environments offers interesting insights into predictably diverse responses to the more standardized intentions of the new National Curriculum.

Whiteside (1978) suggests that there is a tendency to treat educational innovations as products to be introduced into a school, as technological innovations are introduced into an industrial plant. The value conflicts which surround the idea of educational change are treated superficially or even ignored. In my research it was soon apparent that an innovation could not be viewed as a reified entity having an object existence independent of the adopter's perceptions or construction of reality. Shared values could not be assumed. What was finally implemented reflected the individual teacher's personal construction in terms of their own values within a particular social context. Fullan (1989, p. 193) comments:

> assume that one of the main purposes of the process of implementation is to exchange your reality of what should be through

interaction with implementers and others concerned. Stated another way, assume that successful implementation consists of some
transformation or continual development of initial ideas ... any
significant innovation requires individual implementers to work
out their own meaning.

While teaching is an eclectic activity, the study of the two schools demonstrated a fundamental philosophical divide which generated differing aims
and emphases in the classroom. The expressions of conflict and change
were different in the two schools but the central pivot around which the
study ultimately revolved was ideological — the differing views of knowledge derived from differing views of the nature of schooling and of
education itself (Dalton, 1988). Commenting on a recent statement by a
Senior HMI that to confuse the description of a curriculum and its design,
with its delivery is a fatal flaw, Armstrong (1990) comments:

the error lies rather in the metaphor of delivery itself. It implies
that knowledge is a commodity or artefact which can be passed
from teacher to pupil, old to young in a relatively uncomplicated
way. But knowledge is not independent of the means by which
it is transmitted, as the metaphor of delivery would entice us
to suppose.

In an earlier statement Armstrong went to the heart of the argument — 'My
contention is that the process of education should imply a dynamic relationship between teacher, pupil and task out which knowledge is recon-
structed, for both teacher and pupil in the light of a shared experience'
(1977, p. 86). Such an interpretation sees the real curriculum as achievements resulting from pupils' engagement and learning in schools rather
than an uncomplicated list of targets of knowledge and skills.

Recent developments in the National Curriculum have sharpened the
knowledge debate. Initially, for example, 'Knowing' in the music curriculum was separated from the other three major curriculum activities: Performing; Composing and Listening.

This map of musical knowledge falls into the trap that enticed
other subject groups, the failure to recognise that activities and
learning outcomes are two different but related dimensions ... to
isolate 'knowing' as one attainment target in the same dimension
as activities is to encourage a false view of knowledge as merely
professional, factual; whereas skills and attitudes are crucial to
knowing in the arts. . . . The epistemological model here is crystal
clear and profoundly wrong. Musical knowledge is made a travesty
by being completely split off from musical activities and is con-
fined to the facts of history and theory (Swanwick, 1992).

Later negotiations linked understanding with performing and composing thus moving closer to Whitty's assertion (1974, p. 120), 'Knowledge is seen as inextricably linked to methods of coming to know and any supposed dichotomy between them is therefore false'.

Glaserfeld (1989) rejects a simple transferable view of knowledge contrasting it with a view of the child as actively engaged in the construction of knowledge if meaningful learning is to take place.

> At the basis of the constructivist theory of knowing is first of all the idea that knowledge is not an iconic representation of an external environment or world but rather a mapping of ways of acting and thinking that are viable in that they have proven helpful to the subject in attaining experimental goals.

The GYSL Project — common to the two schools

The original published materials for teachers and pupils addressed contemporary issues of leisure, work and urban living. The *Teacher Guides* adopted a rational curriculum planning model in which objectives in terms of key ideas, skills and attitudes and values were outlined as the basis for illustrative content. The objectives however, in contrast to those of Bloom, were non-behavioural and imprecise. The skills indicated directions for improvement rather than specific goals to achieve. The key ideas objectives were based on 'the structure of a field of knowledge' (Stenhouse, 1975) rather than on performance level objectives. The project was clearly influenced by the 'new geography' movement, reflected in the emphasis on ideas and theories rather than descriptive facts, in the search for patterns and processes. The project sought to answer questions about the real world.

It aimed to encourage active methods of learning with 'full pupil involvement and participation' and 'by seeking answers to problems, individual thinking is encouraged and this replaces memorisation as the dominant classroom activity'. The activities, however, were intended to 'lead to the achievement of stated objectives' largely through guided discovery approaches. The project felt it was breaking new ground by focusing on controversial issues within a social and political context promoting discussion, problem-solving and simulation type approaches (*Geography for the Young School Leaver*, Nelson, 1975a).

The purpose of the research

Certain key questions were formulated at an early stage —

1   What was the nature of the actual classroom learning experience of the pupils?

2   Where was the GYSL project located within the varying ideological
     stances of the school's curriculum?
3   In what ways did the cultural norms of the school influence learn-
     ing activities in the classroom and vice versa?
4   What were the processes that inhibited or facilitated change?

Locations

Deansby — a large well-established mixed 11–16 secondary modern
            school in an inner urban area.
Birchwood — a medium-size mixed 11–16 high school set in an afflu-
            ent rural commuter area.

Methodology

The researcher spent the major part of a year in the two schools mainly as
an observer, occasionally contributing as a teacher colleague. Further data
was collected in the next two years. It was instructive to examine complex
interactions as the GYSL project was implemented in two social systems,
and so explore the interpretation of this innovation in the classroom, taking
as the starting point 'practice rather than precept' — regarding 'the learning
milieu as containing the substance of curriculum innovation, not as often
implied, its pale or distorted shadow' (Hamilton, 1976).

A form of ethnographic research was adopted in which the operation
of innovations could be seen and experienced in their natural settings. A
response could be made to issues identified as the salient ones as far as the
actors were concerned. The research, following the new sociology, was
concerned with 'how the actors construct the social world through interpretation and action' (Woods and Hammersley, 1977, p. 11). The research
techniques were varied — direct observation in the classroom, informal
discussions, as well as taped 'formal' interviews with pupils and staff. By
both observation and discussion rather than by questionnaire the researcher
observed and analyzed both classroom performance and teachers' stated
intentions. Taken-for-granted understandings were brought under scrutiny.
Detailed transcripts of tapes and a draft analysis were read over and discussed with leading participants. At a later stage in the research a contract
was drawn up with the schools which clarified the ownership of the data
collected. Both the data and its interpretation were open to scrutiny by any
member of staff.

Originally the Verbal Interaction Category System devised by Amidon
and Hunter (1967) for classroom observation was to be used exclusively.
However, while the analysis gave a precise picture of the balance and
structure of the interaction it proved to be restrictive. It did not reflect the

dynamics of a lesson or one's personal impression of it. A similar criticism was made by Delamont (1976, p. 28) when she experienced a lesson in which a casual comment conveyed an important shared meaning between pupils and staff. In this research the Interaction System was used for parts of lessons but generally a more open approach based on a check list in *Looking Behind the Classroom Door* (Goodlad and Klein, 1974) was favoured.

1   Milieu — as a home for children, is the classroom welcoming and stimulating? Is the teacher supportive?
2   Instructional Activity — does the teacher relate to the children's present knowledge and experience of the topic? Is the teacher the source of knowledge to groups or individuals?
3   Subject Matter — What do the other children do with it? Do they relate it to other experiences/subjects?
4   Materials and Equipment — Is it adequate? Up to date?
5   Involvement — how involved is/are the teacher/children?
6   Interaction — teacher to child, child to teacher, exchanging ideas with each other, where do ideas come from?
7   Inquiry — the process of learning; seeking out or learning conclusions?
8   Independence — freedom, control, who asks whom?
9   Curriculum Balance — across fields of knowledge, modified according to the needs of the class.
10 Ceilings — and floors — of expectancy.

Deansby School

> *'The Project's in cardboard boxes — the kids fill in what they can'*

By accompanying Year 8 and Year 10 classes over a week of their curriculum it was possible to get a clearer impression of the school context in which the geography staff operated. Much of the work of the school was traditional, often didactic. Many of the classes reflected characteristics of the 'Collected Code' (Bernstein, 1971), typified by firm boundaries between subjects and high teacher control over the selection, organization and pacing of the knowledge transmitted and received in the pedagogical relationship. A Year 10 Science lesson serves to illustrate. Here is a summary:

> The lesson was in the Science laboratory. The pupils were seated at benches. The topic was exposure of skin to variations of temperature and humidity.

1.45   A video was switched on almost immediately. Only the title of the lesson was given.
2.17   A period of teacher talk in which no questions were asked or received. Towards the end of the lesson, the pupils were asked to draw the outline of their palm on a page, then to insert areas of sensitivity.
2.45   No summary of final discussion. End of lesson.

Comment:

There was no attempt to link with personal experience, e.g. problems of camping on holiday. The pupils made no active contribution. It was a perfect example of 'School Knowledge' rather than 'Active Knowledge' (Barnes, 1976), and of strong framing partly in terms of teacher selection and organization of framing, partly in terms of teacher selection and organization of knowledge, but also in terms of the strength of the boundary between the everyday community knowledge of the pupils and educational knowledge. The pupils here exercised no control in the formulation of knowledge in the classroom.

The geography staff, anxious to move away from a dominant transmission model and develop more flexible and active approaches were only too aware of the effect teaching in other parts of the school had on the pupils. One said:

There ought to be more of a discussion element in geography but we were held back by unresponsive behaviour — the pupils do not respond easily or well. They have become conditioned. They are not expected to discuss or give their views.

Another commented — 'The youngsters seem at a loss when new methods are tried. They expect to be quiet. They expect to be told'. The geographers could not simply impose a new regime. There had to be negotiation (Rudduck, 1991).

How then did the geographers respond, when furnished with the project's new approaches to geography teaching and an extensive range of multimedia resource materials? Of many geography lessons seen with project groups, 75 per cent were based on worksheets. I had not initially realized the significance of the remark: 'The project's in cardboard boxes — the kids fill in what they can'. The head of geography, Ken Newman had introduced the project into his department. He was regarded by the head teacher as a curriculum pathfinder. Ken realized that the project would have a disturbing effect on some members of the department who saw their subject largely in content/transmissive terms. Change would bring with it 'initially at least, the burdens of incompetence' (Stenhouse, 1975, p. 169). New skills would have to be rapidly acquired. So for Ken the worksheet was a method of relaying and interpreting the project to his staff — it would serve as an in-service medium in the transitional period. Many of the worksheets were well thought out. They introduced new content and new skills. For example in *People, Places and Work* (Geography for the Young School Leaver, 1975b) the topic 'worker migration' was explored. There were comprehension questions requiring the transformation of data (Bloom *et al.*, 1956). For example:

- draw a bar graph to show the percentage of foreign workers employed in European countries in 1972.

There were also questions seeking pupil opinions and judgments. For example:

- should we regard migrant workers as full members of the community with equal rights to public services or merely as people working in the country for a short period with no such rights? Give reasons for your answer.

The work was highly individual although not individualized. It was a kind of guided discovery approach to learning yet generally ensuring reproduction rather than the production of knowledge. The worksheet acted as a control mechanism. As there was no social interaction the learner was isolated. The teacher was thus less responsive to the pupils as individuals than in face-to-face interaction. The worksheet approach meant that the initiatives and choices were in the teacher's hands. The questions were the teacher's not the pupils'. Also by curtailing collaborative learning it suggested a form of curriculum development which devalued teacher and pupil collaboration. A similar pattern was observed in the conduct of fieldwork. The hypotheses were given by the teacher. Ken could claim that he had moved away from a simple transmission reception mode with its characteristic emphasis on programmes of subject matter to be covered (for example, learning geography through accumulating facts and practising skills). Yet clearly the teacher was still in firm control of both the selection and methods of transmission of knowledge. In many ways the worksheet continued a transmission approach. Goodson (1976) includes a broad spectrum of teaching styles — chalk and talk, question and answer, individualized worksheets, even discovery projects in a transmission approach if this is characterized 'as an educational incident which sets the learning of knowledge previously planned or defined by the teacher as the basic objective'. An observer of the project rightly questioned how far was the change of content by real pedagogic change?

Birchwood School

This school contrasts with Deansby in many ways. It is a purpose built comprehensive school serving an agricultural community/middle-class commuter village. The staff appointed to the new school were generally younger than those at Deansby. The humanities department in which the geography project was implemented was led by an able teacher, supported by an articulate deputy head, with a strong commitment to a process model of the curriculum (Parker and Rubin, 1966). These two formed the 'radical' wing of the department. The deputy head had recently completed his MA at the University of East Anglia and was clearly much influenced by the ideas of Lawrence Stenhouse. Within the humanities department the project was promoted and defended by 'reformed geographers' but derided as reactionary by the progressive radicals, led by the head of department, who questioned the logic of a subject-based approach which for them was essentially a new form of content. The official departmental view of the project was thus deeply sceptical, viewing objectives as representative of a more behaviouristic approach to knowledge. Worksheets were rejected!

Their humanities syllabus stated that 'the curriculum is seen not in terms of behavioural objectives but in terms of principles of procedure. These principles are not pre-specified targets at which teaching is aimed but criteria of judgment which help teachers get the 'process' of learning right'.

The radicals sought to exemplify the principles of the Bruner, Man, a Course of Study Project (MACOS) which was used with the younger years. Its implementation caused considerable pain and conflict in the department but its influence on the pupils' classroom experience led to profound changes in pedagogy. Keith Yates, head of the humanities department, commented that MACOS explores key concepts such as learning, dependency, aggression, social organization, communication (a higher order than the key ideas proposed in GYSL) —

> It is open-ended, never finished. It gets kids raising their own questions and deciding where they want to go. I don't know where it is going to end. When I start a communication lesson as a part of a geography unit, I know where it is going to end. This could be just as exciting, just as stimulating. It all depends how you view learning, what you think is important at the end of the day. If we take a theme like 'Children at War', let's not make it content based, not learning about the last war primarily, but looking at children's experience and getting empathy between then and now. Ideally start with the seven instrumental or pedagogic aims from MACOS. These really sum up my ideas of education. They also sum up what this department stands for:
>
> 1 to initiate and develop in youngsters a process of question posing (the enquiry method);
> 2 to teach a research methodology where children can look for information to answer questions they have raised;

3   to help youngsters develop the ability to use a variety of sources, first, second and third-hand, as evidence from which to develop hypotheses and draw conclusions;
4   to conduct classroom discussions in which youngsters learn to listen to others as well as express their own ideas;
5   to legitimize the search; that is, to give sanction and support to open-handed discussions where definite answers to many questions are not found;
6   to encourage children to reflect on their own experiences;
7   to create a new role for the teacher in which he/she becomes a resource rather than an authority.

As he saw it, geography colleagues in the humanities department were resistant to the process approach in education. They were more at ease with the geography project. They saw it as having a well-defined structure while allowing them to develop more open methods of learning. Certainly the content planning meetings, team teaching and intense discussion led to a very different interpretation of GYSL than that at Deansby. Classroom work was far more interactive with genuine group activities involving discussion, role play and problem solving. It was apparent too, in the geography fieldwork, where in the student projects the hypotheses were generated by the pupils and the responsibility was upon them to conduct the investigation using a research methodology similar to that proposed by Bruner.

The strategies used in a lower school visit to the Vikings Exhibition in London illustrated a fundamentally different approach from that of Deansby. The historian said:-

I am trying to get away from worksheets. I believe in a high degree of oral exchange starting from the pupil, asking them which are the things they want to know about a Viking village. When the traditional worksheet is finished at an exhibition the pupil may think 'That's all I need to do — I have "done" the exhibition'.

The Birchwood pupils' hypotheses help to focus and sharpen a child's perception and direct his energies towards a real discovery learning. The hypotheses were formulated in a classroom discussion prior to the visit. There were discussions in groups with a strong emphasis on cooperative endeavour rather than a highly individualized approach. A lot of time was spent in these groups talking through the preparation. Such hypotheses as 'The Vikings were all pagans' were typical. In discussion the pupils were asked to:

Discuss a plan of action and discuss the sort of evidence you need to look for on a trip. Who will look out for what? How will you present your findings? Now write your hypotheses in your general notebook making sure you take it with you on your trip. In it, collect any notes that might help to prove your hypotheses.

The work undertaken by the pupils at the London Museum was purposeful, involving them in detective approaches as they scanned many parts of the exhibition in their search for evidence. It was their responsibility to select or discard evidence to support or reject their hypotheses. There was no tidy end to the exercise as there might have been with a straightforward 'observe and record' kind of worksheet. Back in the classroom, the cooperative work continued with pupils, provers and disprovers of the hypotheses, putting their results together. The two groups were asked to reach a conclusion. The onus throughout was on the pupils to research, organize, present and evaluate their results.

The 'radicals' in the humanities department felt that the stated key ideas of the geographers had become for them the new content. Without a radical change in their view of pedagogy the ideas would be taught in a transmissive mode. The GYSL innovation could therefore become assimilated into fairly traditional classroom practices because the radicals argued 'its content was in essence congruent with the culturally embedded epistemological assumptions of geography teachers' (Blenkin, Edwards and Kelly, 1992, p. 46). Another practical example illustrates the point. In a settlement topic the geographers began with a carefully itemized list of key ideas towards which the pupils under their direction would work in a 'guided discovery' approach. The radicals produced a much more pupil-centred approach. Keith Yates, Head of Humanities:

I would probably start with a settlement game — what questions would it raise? Look at historical place names. Then give the kids the task of producing a town trail. Do not feed the answers, leave the questions to them. Groups could focus on the station, the green, pubs, cricket club using a wide range of documentary evidence, books, archive material. Here is another idea. At one time Birchwood was to have become an overspill area for the GLC, say a plan for 40,000 people. I would show slides of Harlow as stimulus material and talk about new towns. Then I would say to the group. 'You are a pressure group. I want you to make a case against this by using all the resources available. Make your own trail with written material, slides etc. convey something of what Birchwood is. . . . they would at the end have learned an awful lot of history, geography and social science — but above all they would become involved in the process of learning' (Dalton, 1988).

The model was far closer to an 'Integrated Code' (Bernstein, 1971). The 'radical' teachers gave the pupils a much greater degree of control over the organization, pacing and timing of knowledge and to a certain extent, the selection of knowledge than did the geographers, although these were more radical than the Deansby geographers. The humanities department at Birchwood was generally weak on the 'frame' scale. The radical teachers saw the GYSL Project with its specific framework of ideas, suggested methodology and its predetermined evaluation procedures as being strong on the framing scale. In radical vein, the deputy head wrote:

> The teacher is no longer simply the authoritative imparter of knowledge, the decider of issues, but is acting as a consultant, a guide, a resource bank, a stimulator of questions. He is a person who will be primarily interested in what the pupil is thinking and doing.

The GYSL Project was being scrutinized and implemented in a very different way from that at Deansby School.

Conclusion

The two departments implementing a common curriculum created very different classroom learning experiences for the pupils. The diversity was related especially to two main areas:

i)   the personal values and philosophy that the individual teachers brought to their interpretation of the curriculum proposal;
ii) the immediate cultural context in which they were working. Lacey (1977) refers to the 'intersection between biography and situation' as a useful basis of analysis of an individual's actions or strategies.

The deputy head at Birchwood School identified one dimension of difference as being a continuum between:-

Stress on means/process		Stress on ends/content
Principles of procedure	————————	then decide efficient
Content as a vehicle		and effective means

Certainly their humanities staff could be 'mapped' along the continuum. The radicals rejected a traditional model in which intellectual knowledge is only discovered by experts and the pupils' job is seen as retaining this knowledge and becoming skilled in approved ways of manipulating it. Were echoes of that seen in the approach to worksheets at Deansby? The radicals challenged these assumptions in their move towards a constructivist theory of knowing. Knowledge was not a commodity to be conveyed or instilled but was essentially the result of an individual's constructive activity (Glaserfeld, 1989). Clearly the educational process will take a variety of forms including instruction and training, but centre stage will be initiation —

> to teach a discipline or field of knowledge is always to 'teach' the epistemology of that discipline, the nature of its tenure on knowledge (Rudduck and Hopkins, 1985).

In examining our pedagogic assumptions the 'Primary Education in Leeds' report urges avoidance of conformist cultures which elevate particular classroom practices as ends in themselves. The emphasis should be on the goals and processes of learning (Alexander, 1992).

The culture or ethos of the school plays a key role in any change in classroom practice. In Deansby School the pressure to conform to established norms of learning and teaching was considerable. It had a pervasive conditioning effect on pupil attitudes and expectations. In Birchwood the humanities department met with criticism and antagonism from other subject departments suspicious of the process curriculum. The involvement and support of the deputy head was critical in sustaining their classroom strategies. Holly (1986) argues that every innovation has to be filtered within and screened by the culture of the school. Some cultures will neutralize the impact of change, others will learn from and accommodate new ideas. Rudduck develops this idea 'in the power of the existing culture of the school and classroom to accommodate, absorb and expel innovations that are at odds with the dominant structures and values that hold habit in place' (1986, p. 7).

One key to successful change in classroom practice must therefore be as Fullan suggests — to think not so much of innovation in the school but innovation of the school (1985).

References

ALEXANDER, R. (1992) *Primary Education in Leeds. Briefing and summary*, Leeds School of Education.

AMIDON, E. and HUNTER, E. (1967) *Improving Teaching: The Analysis of Verbal Interaction*, London, Holt, Rinehert and Winston.

ARMSTRONG, M. (1977) 'Restructuring Knowledge' in WATTS, J. (Ed.) *The Countesthorpe Experience*, London, Allen & Unwin.

ARMSTRONG, M. (1990) 'Does the National Curriculum rest on a mistake?' in EVERTON, T., MAYNE, P. and WHITE, S. *Effective Learning into a New ERA*, Jessica Kingsley.

BARNES, D. (1976) *From Communication to Curriculum*, Harmondsworth, Penguin.

BECHER, T. (1989) 'The National Curriculum and the implementation gap', in PREEDY, M., *Approaches to Curriculum Management*, Milton Keynes, Open University.

BERNSTEIN, B. (1971) 'On the classification and framing of educational knowledge', in YOUNG, M.F.D. (Ed.), *Knowledge and Control*, Collier Macmillan.

BLENKIN, G.M., EDWARDS, G. and KELLY, A.V. (1992) *Change and the Curriculum*, Paul Chapman.

BLOOM, B.S. *et al.* (1956) *Taxonomy of Educational Objectives, I*, London, Longman.

DALTON, T.H. (1988) *The Challenge of Curriculum Innovation*, Lewis, Falmer Press.

DELAMONT, S. (1976) *Interaction in the Classroom*, London, Methuen.

FULLAN, M. (1985) 'Change processes and strategies at the local level', *Elementary School Journal*, **85**, 3.

FULLAN, M. (1989) 'Planning doing and coping with change', in MOON, B. and MURPHY, P., *Policies for the Curriculum*, London, Hodder & Stoughton.

GEOGRAPHY FOR THE YOUNG SCHOOL LEAVER (1975a) Teacher Guide, London, Nelson.

GEOGRAPHY FOR THE YOUNG SCHOOL LEAVER (1975b) People Place and Work, London, Nelson.

GLASERSFELD, E. (1989) 'Learning as a Constructive Activity', in MURPHY, P. and MOON, B., *Developments in Learning and Assessment*, London, Hodder & Stoughton.

GOODLAD, J.I. and KLEIN, P. (1974) *Looking Behind the Classroom Door*, Charles A Jones.

GOODSON, I.F. (1976) 'Towards an alternative pedagogy', in WHITTY, G. and YOUNG, M., *Explorations in the Politics of School Knowledge*, Driffeld Nafferton Books.

HAMILTON, D. (1976) *Curriculum Evaluation*, London, Open Books.

HOLLY, P.J. (1986) 'Soaring like turkeys: The impossible dream?' *School Organisation*, **6**, 3.

LACEY, C. (1977) *The Socialisation of Teachers*, London, Methuen.

PARKER, J.A. and RUBIN, L.J. (1966) *Process as Content: Curriculum Design and the Application of Knowledge*, Rand McNally.

RUDDUCK, J. and HOPKINS, D. (1985) Research as a Basis for Teaching: Readings from the Work of Lawrence Stenhouse, London, Heinemann.

RUDDUCK, J. (1986) *Understanding Curriculum Change. Division of Education*, University of Sheffield.

RUDDUCK, J. (1991) *Innovation and Change*, Milton Keynes, Open University.

STENHOUSE, L. (1975) *An Introduction to Curriculum Research and Development*, London, Heinemann.

SWANWICK, K. (1992) 'The Key of Knowledge', *TES*, 13 March 1992.

WHITESIDE, T. (1978) *The Sociology of Educational Innovations*, London, Methuen.

WHITTY, G. (1974) 'Sociology and the problem of radical change', in FLUDE, M. and AHIER, J. (Ed.) *Educability, Schools and Ideology*, London, Croom Helm.

WOODS, P. and HAMMERSLEY, M. (1977) *School Experience*, London, Croom Helm.

5 The Impact of the National Curriculum on Planning for Classroom Science

Steve Farrow

The introduction of the National Curriculum was heralded as the greatest educational reform of the century. The political rhetoric was of educational entitlement for all pupils, with the stated aim of 'raising standards'.

Significantly perhaps, non-maintained schools, and those in Scotland and Northern Ireland, were excepted from the requirement to implement the National Curriculum in 1989. The maintained schools of England and Wales were to be the places where a state-defined knowledge-based curriculum, backed by the force of law, would be introduced in order to raise educational standards.

The passage of a law which states that something must or should happen is, of course, no guarantee that it will — particularly when its import represents a source of disagreement among the people who will be involved in its implementation.

It may be that history will record the introduction of the National Curriculum as a classic example of such a case. The combination of factors which accompanied its introduction — the apparently deliberate ignoring of the opinions of education professionals, the perceived sham of the consultation process, the indecent haste with which the whole initiative was introduced, and the content overload, particularly for primary school curricula — all contributed to a sense of bewilderment and despair which affected all classroom teachers to some extent or other. But teachers are traditionally resilient people, accustomed to accommodating change in practice, and many saw the introduction of the National Curriculum as an opportunity rather than as a threat to their practice. It was also an excellent opportunity to track the effects of a curriculum initiative (in this case, a non-optional one!).

One of the most threatening areas of the curriculum for primary teachers is that of science. The requirements of the National Curriculum, which awarded science the status of a core subject, ostensibly equivalent to English and mathematics, caused great concern in primary circles. The implementation of the requirements of the science NC presented problems for many teachers in terms of subject knowledge, and for many schools in terms of policy and resources.

This chapter describes the progress of a small scale research project designed to monitor the effects of the National Curriculum on the changing provision for science in primary school classrooms, and reports findings from the first four academic years of the study.

Background to the project

The project used as a 'window' into primary classrooms, the experience of fourth year teacher training students during their final block teaching practice placements. Fourth-year Primary B.Ed. students at the University of Sunderland are required to teach 75 per cent of a full timetable during their final block practice. They are expected to take on the role of a class teacher, and to be able to deal with the whole of the primary curriculum.

The major assumption made with relevance to the survey, was that schools would continue to operate their policies with respect to curriculum planning, and would not substantially alter what they were doing because the people 'in charge' of the classrooms were student teachers. The science required from the students could thus be seen as a reflection of the schools' policies, and not simply as a 'fill-in' for the duration of the practice. This assumption is supported by a trend which has been noticeable during the past three years, which is that schools have become increasingly prescriptive about the curriculum content required of student teachers. This is unsurprising in view of the requirements now laid upon schools by the detail of the National Curriculum.

The survey

The project takes the form of an iterative survey, designed as applicable to successive fourth-year student cohorts. The intention has been to compile data about the emphases placed on different models of curriculum planning for science in primary schools, in the hope of tracing any changes to such planning evident during the years following the introduction of the National Curriculum.

The survey takes the form of a questionnaire in three sections. The first part is designed to find out the age distribution of classes taught. The second section asks respondents to match the science teaching required of them against a list of descriptors, and the third section asks students to categorize their perception of science policy and planning in the school concerned.

Results and discussion

The results are presented as summaries of the data derived from four successive cohorts of Year 4 students. They represent 'snapshots' of four academic years and were collected in March 1990, December 1990, December 1991 and December 1992.

Science in the classrooms

So, what science has been happening in the classrooms as a result of the introduction of the science National Curriculum? What changes have been taking place in terms of the way science is being planned? The table below summarizes the results from four cohorts of students, who were asked to match their experiences on final teaching practice against a set of descriptors of 'science requirements'.

Table 5.1   Classification of classroom science requirements

Category	3/90	12/90	12/91	12/92
A. Do anything you like	9	7	9	9
B. Choose any part of an already planned topic	18	24	24	21
C. Do a particular part of an already planned topic	10	8	8	21
D. Do a particular AT	6	6	7	8
E. Do part of a particular AT	2	2	1	3
F. Do a particular S o A	3	0	1	1
G. Other	0	2	1	2
Total	48	49	51	65

With respect to the science teaching expected of fourth-year students, the survey has indicated that for the academic year 1989–90, most schools tended to include science as part of a topic or theme and 28/48 responses showed that the schools concerned had planned themes or topics for the spring term, and the students were expected to play a part in their implementation. This is perhaps an indication that primary schools in general were continuing to promote what they believed to be good practice, and were matching the science National Curriculum to their theme and topic planning rather than the other way round.

Conversely, it appears that a small number of schools were actually gearing their teaching directly to attainment targets (8/48), and even fewer were targeting specific statements of attainment — 'teaching to the test' — (3/48). Whilst the tendency to retain theme and topic teaching may well have been a pre-Alexandrian cause for comfort, it would be as well to acknowledge that this sample was biased towards the upper age range of primary schools, and it may well be that the full burden of the statutory requirements had not yet fallen on the classes concerned.

Although the second set of data were gathered in the same calendar year, they represent findings from a different school year (the December date was because of a change in the timing of the final block practice on the course concerned). Perhaps the most startling indication from a comparison of the December 1990 data with those of the previous year, is how little appears to have changed. Apart from the targeting of particular statements of attainment (which seems to have disappeared), the science requirements were much as before.

Similarly, the data from December 1991, gathered more than two years after the initiation of the National Curriculum in schools, presents a pattern similar to those of previous years. Perhaps this is merely an indication of the extent to which topic work is rooted in the curriculum planning of primary schools. It may also be an indication of the unwillingness, or inability, of schools to tackle science as a discipline in its own right. Teachers will naturally shy away from areas of the curriculum in which they feel a lack of confidence, and a simple strategy to accommodate science would be to absorb it into topic-based teaching.

Finally, in 1992 there seems to have been more direction of students towards particular parts of topics already planned. This is possibly because schools are now planning to match their teaching more tightly to the requirements of the National Curriculum. There seems to be less 'leeway' with respect to the science requirements.

One overall conclusion appears to present itself however, namely that the requirements of the science National Curriculum appear to have had little effect on the way in which science has been planned in primary schools in the years since its introduction.

Schools' policies for Primary Science

What have been the methods of curriculum planning used by the schools, and have they adapted their planning in any way to accommodate the requirements of the National Curriculum? Again, students were asked to match their perceptions of the schools' approach to curriculum policy and planning, and a summary of the data is presented in Table 5.2.

Table 5.2 Perceptions of schools' science policy

Category	3/90	12/90	12/91	12/92
H. Whole school agreed theme or topic	9	7	6	8
I. Year or class based	30	29	32	44
J. Based on a formulated policy				
1. Theme or topic with ATs clustered round theme	10	12	6	12
2. Individual ATs targeted	2	3	4	8
3. Individual S o A targeted	1	0	0	0
4. Other	0	3	4	1

In terms of general planning, whole-school models are relatively uncommon. The large majority of schools seem to undertake their planning for science on a year or class basis. The initial concern expressed over the National Curriculum simply becoming a 'shopping list' appears to be unfounded, although there is a small tendency for an increase in AT-specific planning across the four data sets. This may be because of an increasing awareness in schools of the need to 'target' individual ATs which may slip through the topic 'net'.

It is perhaps surprising in spite of continuous exhortation from DFE and NCC to develop whole school policies for science, that such a relatively small proportion of schools were perceived as having a formulated policy of any kind (category J1–4). It may be that schools have developed such policies, but that they are 'invisible' in terms of student awareness. Conversely, at least one student reported that the existence of the NC Science 'ring binder' was invoked as proof of the existence of a school policy for science. Perhaps not surprisingly in view of the classroom requirements for science, the outstanding feature of the data appears to be the relative lack of change from year to year. The proportions of responses devoted to 'topic-based' and 'AT-based' planning have remained remarkably similar.

A summary of comparisons between the three sets of data is presented as Table 5.3.

Table 5.3 Comparisons between years

Curriculum Delivery	MARCH 1990	DEC. 1990	DEC. 1991	DEC. 1992
Topics/Themes	28/48	32/49	32/51	42/65
ATs	8/48	8/49	8/51	11/65
S o As	3/48	0/49	1/51	1/65
Curriculum Planning				
Year/Class Based	30/52	29/54	32/52	44/73
Formulated Policy	13/52	18/54	14/52	21/73

The status of science in primary schools

One of the interesting outcomes of the successive annual surveys has been the changing status of science in the classrooms, as indicated by the time made available for science on a weekly basis.

During the first year of the survey, responses to enquiries about time availability were anecdotal, as they derived from discussion sessions. Latterly, a more rigorous attempt has been made to quantify the time devoted to science in classrooms.

In Year 2 of the survey (December 1990), it transpired from discussion that in a sample of twenty-three classrooms, science accounted for anything from one to five hours per week. In Year 3 (December 1991), the

Table 5.4 Time per week devoted to science — December 1991 (n = 33)

Hours per Week	1	2	3	4
No. of Classrooms	4	9	13	7

Table 5.5 Time per week devoted to science — December 1992 (n = 59)

Hours per week	.5	1	1.5	2	2.5	3	4	5	6
No. of Classrooms	1	7	6	25	3	7	3	5	2

range had narrowed to one to four hours per week, with sample distribution as per Table 5.4.

From the table it can be calculated that the mean time devoted to science in the classrooms concerned in the sample was two hours forty minutes. Those classrooms dedicating four hours per week to science were using 17.0 per cent of available time (assuming a notional school week of 23.5 hours).

By December 1992, the mean time devoted to science in the classrooms sampled had decreased to two hours twenty-seven minutes. The sample distribution is shown in Table 5.5.

Although the range of time allocation has increased for the 1992 data, the modal figure has dropped from three hours in 1991 to two hours in 1992. This is perhaps not surprising in view of the other, and increasing pressures on curriculum time, but it is disturbing with respect to the status of science as a core subject.

Data from a separate survey support these findings and also point to the disparity in time allocation between the core subjects in primary schools. In February 1993, twenty-four primary school teachers were asked to estimate the time allocated per week to each of the core subjects in their classrooms. The mean values for each of the subjects were as follows (n = 24):

English	4 hours 53 minutes per week
Mathematics	4 hours 30 minutes per week
Science	2 hours 10 minutes per week

(I am indebted to Helen Richards for the above data)

These data appear to confirm the relative decline in time allocated to science, and indicate that science is, in effect, being treated as a foundation subject, at least as far as time allocation is concerned. The explanation for this effect may lie with the increasing pressure on available time as other foundation subjects come 'on stream'. It may be that time is being created for history and geography, for example, at the expense of science rather than the other core subjects.

If science time continues to dwindle, then scope exists for a serious mismatch between expectations in terms of statutory requirements, and outcomes in terms of assessed ability, particularly if children are being disallowed the time needed to encompass the whole of the given science curriculum. The fault, if any, lies not with the teachers so much as with an overcrowded curriculum, a fact now thankfully acknowledged by nearly all involved in education policy making. Having been promised a National Curriculum which would remain under continuous review, it will be interesting to observe the frequency of any changes which may be made.

In summary, the main points which have emerged from the survey so far are as follows:

- following the first year (1989) 'accommodation' of science into the curriculum, there seems to be little detectable change in the way in which schools have undertaken their curriculum planning for science;
- there appears to be little 'teaching to the test', although analysis of individual returns shows that there was a concentration on ATs in Y5/6 in 1991;
- there has been a small response to the requirement for the production of whole-school science education policies;
- the time devoted to science in primary classrooms is decreasing, and is significantly lower than that allocated to the other core subjects;
- science now seems to be viewed by schools as a foundation (i.e. non-core) subject.

Although the survey is small, and regional (covering six LEAs), it has already provided a fascinating glimpse into the pace and progress of change in primary classrooms, in this case change initiated by major national reform. It is interesting to see that the National Curriculum document has not become a 'shopping list' of curriculum content in science, and that theme and topic work in general still holds sway. It is perhaps a little disturbing however, that many schools seem not yet to have a perceptible science policy.

What will be of particular interest in future will be the attempt to monitor changes in curriculum planning and science teaching in the light of the 'new' attainment targets, the increasing demands for time made by the rest of the statutory curriculum and the changing assessment requirements at Key Stages 1 and 2. The paradox implicit in the ministerial recommendation that primary teaching should be more subject-based, more whole-class based, yet should forswear mixed-ability group work, appears to have gone largely unremarked.

References

DES (1991) *The National Curriculum in Science*, London, HMSO.

Farrow, S. (1992) 'Science in Primary Schools: Will it ever be a core subject?' *The Curriculum Journal*, **3**, pp. 311–314.

Wragg, E.C., Burnett, N. and Carr, C. (1989) 'Primary Teachers and the National Curriculum', *Research Papers in Education*, **4**, 3.

6 Expect the Unexpected: School-specific Contexts and the Shaping of School-based INSET Projects

Ray Chatwin, Paul McGowan, Maggie Turner and Trisha Wick

At first sight, the intention of improving classroom practice seems straightforward. The practitioner evaluates the individual classroom, decides which aspect of practice will receive attention, embarks on an improvement effort, evaluates it and re-starts the cycle. Such a view, also encapsulated in some approaches to school review and development (e.g. McMahon *et al.*, 1984), does not take account of the real complexity of this task; particularly of the need to enable a sustained dialogue to take place between those involved, and the initiation of micropolitical activity which may be perceived as threatening for those concerned. While attention has been drawn to the limitations of diagrammatic representations of change processes, for example that they 'present only the general image of a much more detailed and snarled process' (Fullan, 1982), this has not inhibited the spread of similar models in Local Education Authorities (LEAs) across the country. Indeed, it may fairly be said to have become part of the common sense of a 'systematic' approach to school improvement.

This discussion of school review and development is based on a project undertaken between September 1991 and July 1992. The project was carried out by the four members of the Birmingham Schools' In-Service Unit (SISU); a team whose work spans primary and secondary phases.

The project focused on the management of the curriculum and access to it. The consideration of 'access' stems from a concern for the achievement of *all* pupils, black bilingual, girls, working-class children, and their potential and educability; an assumption that the achievement of pupils is strongly related to what happens to them in the school rather than what happens to them at home. This focus grew out of a previous project which concentrated on developing Year 7 (Y7, eleven to twelve-year-old children) pupils' ability to read for learning in several areas of the curriculum. During the latter project, SISU became increasingly aware that there was no discernible link between the management structures of the school and the curriculum. Posts of responsibility made little sense either to us or to the post-holder, for example, what did 'Key Stage' (KS) co-ordinators actually do? There appeared to be little relationship between the job description, the ritual of interview and appointment and possibility of the post-holder developing any role in relation to the curriculum and learning. Neither was it possible to identify any improvement-orientated function for the Senior Management Team (SMT). In the project evaluation, when asked to identify next steps for the school and then to indicate what support the head of department, deputy and headteacher might provide, respondents were surprisingly vague. The evaluation report suggested that this might be due to all, or some, of the following factors:

- classroom teachers do not know what role middle and senior management play in the school, other than overall control and supervision;
- teachers do not know what actions middle and senior management could take to give support;
- some levels of management, or management structures, are weakly related to the curriculum (or in practice not related at all);
- teachers have no expectation of support from management in general;
- teachers have no expectation of support from particular individuals who are incumbents of specific posts;
- teachers expect to be given leadership rather than asked what form it should take.

Following the identification of these factors, two secondary schools were offered the opportunity to focus on the linkage between a classroom improvement effort of some kind and the management structures, in as direct way as possible. Two management team members from each school would attend an off-site introductory conference (also open to other senior staff in LEA secondary schools as a free-standing conference) and would then be supported in their own school during the development work. The issue would be identified by the school itself and ways of working would be agreed before the school-based work began. Two members of SISU would be assigned to the school and would take part in all aspects of the work including INSET, working group membership, classroom work, documentation and liaison with the headteacher.

The school that is the subject of this case study gave no signs in the early stages of the project of the kinds of unpropitious circumstances which might have alerted participants to the presence of deep-seated problems in the ethos of the school; problems which might have hindered the realization of the aims set out in the introductory outline of the purpose of the project sent to the school, i.e.:

- to focus on school management;
- to provide support for senior staff;
- in particular their curriculum and staff development roles;
- therefore to link management and learning;
- recognizing the influence which management can have on the climate for learning;
- support might help senior staff to resource task groups or working parties in the school;
- classroom work might be undertaken, in order to feed into such discussion forums;
- the process would be intended to enhance the school's capacity for self-evaluation;
- in doing so, it would utilize outside support in optimum ways.

The project was interpreted at once as applying to the work of deputy headteachers. For reasons which were never entirely clear, but may well have been related to the headteacher's perceptions of internal political and personal factors, two of the three deputies were nominated to take the leading roles, one with responsibility for curriculum, the other with responsibility for finance. The third deputy, with responsibility for staff development, was not involved. We ourselves accepted this decision as presumably being in line with the school's needs at that time. A major consideration may have been that the school was on three sites, with the third deputy being responsible for the more distant one, whereas the others were based in the main building.

Other factors were noted at the time as possibly influencing developments:

- the headteacher was relatively new to the school, being in post for just over a term at the start of the project;
- the personalities of the two deputies;
- the attitudes of the two deputies to each other;
- the split site (three in all) and its effects on communication between individuals involved in the project, and on the mechanisms of the school in general;
- the pre-existing relationships between deputies and departments.

It was in the nature of the project that the definition of the curriculum need and focus should be a matter for the school personnel to decide. SISU were to assist the process. In the event, the identification of the need was to prove a protracted exercise, with the SISU playing a central role at each stage. Initially, the agenda was set by the deputy headteacher's (curriculum) assessment of the best way forward as being a focus on oracy in the teaching of mathematics. The imperative for this was that the majority of children in the school were bilingual and that considerable numbers of pupils needed a good deal of help with English. The maths department had already expressed a concern about these types of need, and was the kind of department which would be well placed to handle the demands of this kind of project — a department open to new ideas, used to discussion, and not threatened by the presence of outsiders.

The initial contact with the headteacher and deputies had taken place towards the end of the summer term, and the major decisions about the project's focus were shelved until the autumn. SISU had no contact with the maths department until then. In retrospect this might be seen as symptomatic of problems of communication within the school. At the time, though, SISU's concern was to emphasize the project's focus on the needs of senior staff.

At the start of the autumn term work had to be done, both to re-establish what the project was for, and also to identify what was needed to make it a reality in the school. In particular, (in conjunction with the deputies) contact had to made, as quickly as possible, with the maths department in order to make sure that they were also fully informed about what we had in mind, and why *they* had been 'volunteered'.

At this first meeting it emerged that they had only the vaguest idea of what was afoot, although the curriculum deputy had apparently spoken to the head of department (HOD) about the project. Second, the concern about oracy, as it had been described to us, was *not* one which the department itself appeared to recognize as something about which they were currently concerned. They considered that there had been a time when they had given some collective thought on how to develop pupils' oral skills in maths, but that they had dealt with this to their satisfaction in the context of responding to the demands of GCSE assessment and coursework. This led to the abandonment of what was thought to be their chief interest, and to the identification of a real need — this time as they perceived it.

It was decided to meet the department without senior staff. This was so that the SISU team could explain the purpose of the project, rather than the deputy heads. This was important because of the tension which existed between the head of maths and the deputy head (curriculum). It meant, for example, that the project team was forced into a more leading role than had been anticipated, or wanted, and that SISU effectively pre-empted the deputies dealing with the needs identification issue. Had they been present, it would have been interesting to see how the mismatch of perceptions would have been resolved. As it was, the opportunity was lost.

The discussions with the maths department therefore turned to who SISU was, and what it did. In the course of explaining this, reference was made to the previous project on reading development in Y7, and on how an attempt was made to relate such a general issue to the needs of each subject area. Interest was expressed in how this might be achieved in the case of maths. This interest stemmed from efforts which we had been told the school was making to promote reading among pupils. The upshot was that we arranged to meet the department in order to discuss the opportunities and problems presented in maths for pupils' reading. In the course of this second meeting, it emerged that the department had recently given an arithmetic test to its new Y7 pupils, and that the results were giving cause for concern. An illustration was offered on the basis of the results for one class which happened to be to hand, and in which the class teacher had presented the results broken down into sub-scores for each section of the test. It was noticeable that not all sections were equally well or badly done, and the department was asked if this sort of breakdown was available for all classes. As it was not, they were asked whether it would be worth doing. It was from this chance occurrence that the project was to take its form and focus for this school.

The strategy which emerged was aimed at retaining the central purpose of the project, i.e. to support senior management in activities which directly involved them in staff and curriculum development. The paradox was that, although this direct involvement was ensured, it was only achieved when the direction and impetus was provided from the outside. In effect, rather than *supporting* the senior staff, SISU was *propelling* them.

The following were the major features of the course of action pursued by the project participants:

1   Analysis of the Y7 maths results by section. This revealed certain specific areas of difficulty, rather than the generalized failure that was first claimed. On the basis of this analysis, specific action could be taken by the department, such as paying particular attention to those areas of weakness in the first year syllabus. It was also clear that straightforward 'lack of English' was not the main cause of pupils' difficulties. The main cause of difficulty was whether or not the topic had been taught in primary school, and how much time and attention had subsequently been given to it at both primary and secondary school.

2   Joint action was taken by the core participants in the project, i.e. the two deputies, the head of maths and the second in department, plus two members of SISU. This involved interviewing a selected group of pupils, on the basis of their test results, in order to gather further data about their specific difficulties, interests and prior maths learning. It was largely as a result of this data-gathering that the above conclusions were reached. An activity such as interviewing pupils is hardly an innovation in its own right. Nevertheless, innovation is relative, and it certainly marked a sea-change in the school.

3   Two areas of learning were identified for classroom investigation

and strategies for tackling them were worked out in partnerships involving one deputy and one member of the maths department. Each pair was therefore required to plan together and to evaluate the results of what they had found. Everyone was agreed about the positive and beneficial effects of the process, although the structure and impetus was provided throughout by the two members of SISU.

4 The maths department as a whole was briefed by the head of department and the results of the analysis of the Y7 test were debated. Enough interest was shown to prompt the institution of such an approach for all future testing of the year group. The results were also used formatively in relation to the design of the syllabus and to the teaching of particular classes.

5 As well as feeding the department's discussions, it was felt that the SMT as a whole ought at least to be aware of the implications of what had been done. Once the activities described above had been completed, it was arranged for the deputies to report and assess the impact of the work. The head of department was also invited to the meeting. All three spoke appreciatively of the experience, and what it had achieved. In summary there were a number of significant improvements arising from the project.

Improvements arising from the project

— the deficit view of pupils was undermined by the careful attention paid to work pupils could actually do and the context in which it was produced;

— more informed decision making was possible as a result of the collection of reliable data; in particular, decisions concerning the place of language support and the role of the subject teachers in relation to maths (and by extension in other departments too);

— the absolute necessity for a school, especially its senior management team, not to rely on second-hand information about the pupils it serves; this emerged sharply at the meeting with the full SMT, at which those involved in the project squarely opposed any suggestion that SATs results would eventually make such data as had been collected redundant;

— the re-kindling of interest in the curriculum and classroom matters among the deputies involved, and a sense on the part of the department that learning had been established as a priority item on the school's agenda.

Nevertheless, it should also be said that a number of elements in the strategy did not develop optimally:

— at no time in the project did SISU meet the maths department as a whole, in spite of suggestions, hints and requests to do so;
— rather than diminishing, the central role of SISU in making, maintaining and sustaining contacts between the main participants actually increased in importance; this includes contact and communication between head and deputies, deputies and head of department, head of department and second in department;
— it was not possible to persuade the curriculum deputy, who had oversight of the curriculum working party, and access to all departmental records and reports, to develop a *strategy* for taking the lessons of the project, which she had unequivocally endorsed, forward into other areas of the school, either at department level or on SMT.

What might this experience tell us about changing practice in schools?

1 Much has been made of 'innovation overload' in schools. This is far too blunt an instrument for defining what happens in schools. Innovation is only one element, and it is too easily subsumed under other dynamics, such as change, and especially improvement. What was seen is the true pace of improvement. It is painfully slow, and enormous efforts are needed in order to sustain it.
2 The real nature of needs analysis. There has to be somebody who is equipped to discover what the real need is. It cannot be done by a system, however sophisticated. It will always, therefore, be haphazard across institutions.
3 This degree of chance can be reduced sharply by the optimum use of consultancy.
4 Strategic thinking, planning and action are indispensable, but clearly rare. Which is, presumably, why only 10 per cent of schools manage to translate their plans into effect (DES, 1992).

Is it because learning is so much taken-for-granted in the life of schools that it is so difficult to prioritize? The pace of events provides a never-ending supply of matters which demand attention on the part of those responsible for running schools. There is always something needing to be done. It appears that the project *did* help to make a difference to this sort of situation.

The original intention of the project had been to support senior staff, some of them deputy headteachers, in connecting their work more closely with the classroom, and activities which affected pupil learning outcomes for the better. Throughout, SISU was working in typical rather than in failing schools. We thought that we would have a much less obvious role than in some previous projects and that we would act more as consultants for the work the head and senior staff had in mind. It soon became clear, however, that massive intervention was necessary if any progress was to be made in addressing the concerns stated by the school at the outset. The work also added to our sense of puzzlement about the role of deputy headteachers and other senior postholders in secondary schools, when it comes to their activity in support of school and classroom improvement. We therefore find ourselves in much the same positions as the teachers whose perception of the support role of senior staff we quoted at the beginning of this chapter. We feel that this is nothing to do with personal ineffectiveness, it is simply that the leap required is too great given the prior experience of most deputy heads. The requirement that they change perspective to become what are essentially *tutors* of adult learning is simply insufficiently addressed in their professional preparation for deputy headship. At this point we see no evidence to suggest that their role in respect of improvement is really necessary at all, and we feel that more detailed research is necessary; perhaps some of them are much clearer about this aspect of their work, better able to act on it and to play a crucial role in their schools than many of their colleagues. Greater insight is needed into the ways in which this may be done.

There is much in this chapter which is contrary to received wisdom. The current trend towards 'systematic' planning and development is an approach which ignores vital human factors; the approach encouraged was a systematic one, but one which took full account of the nature of the task in which we were engaged and especially of the context, the kind of institution, in which we were working. The common-sensical notion that a school can unproblematically identify its own needs and then meet them with the minimum of external support is again challenged by our work. In our experience, competent consultancy which combines operational involvement and propulsion is essential. Where LEA support services are now simply brought in by schools as they feel the need (or are able to afford them), this constitutes a serious weakening of the school improvement support system (Loucks-Horsley and Crandall, 1986) which should, as we have argued elsewhere (Chatwin *et al.*, 1990), be developing in an entirely different direction.

The experience of this project, and the work of SISU in general, leads us to doubt the capacity of secondary schools and especially of their senior staff, to maintain the consistent focus and marshalling of effort required to bring about real improvement at classroom level. There is a constant struggle to withstand the tendency to allow things to quietly slip away, to fall behind, to cancel or postpone vital meetings in the face of fast moving 'events'. Each time, the role of the team members in keeping the improvement work on course was indispensable to the progress made. Again, this is contrary to the received view that schools can do it all themselves, that they have no need of outside 'experts'. On the contrary, support for school and classroom improvement is an area of expertise to which schools must have access and the tensions which may appear from time to time are indicative that meaningful, rather than cosmetic, change is taking place.

The case study presented illustrates the ragged, messy and sometimes shambolic nature of real — in this case adult — learning taking place; learning about schools as places where learning must constantly be re-stated as the central issue, learning about what needs changing and how it can be changed for the better. As with all learning, the right kind of help, at the right time and in the right quantity, constitutes the scaffolding which senior staff and teachers must have if they are to improve pupils' classroom experiences and raise their attainment.

References

CHATWIN, R., MCGOWAN, P., TURNER, M. and WICK, T. (1990) 'The case for a new kind of LEA support team', *Cambridge Journal of Education*, **20**, 2.

CONSTABLE, H., WILLIAMS, R., BROWN, R., LUDLOW, R. and TAGGART, L. (1986) *An Evaluation of GRIDS in Leeds*, University of Leeds, School of Education.

DEPARTMENT OF EDUCATION AND SCIENCE (1992) *Education in England 1990–91*, The Annual Report of HM Senior Chief Inspector of Schools.

FULLAN, M. (1982) *The Meaning of Educational Change*, New York, Teachers College Press, Columbia University.

GRAY, J. and JESSON, D. (1990) 'The Negotiation and Construction of Performance Indicators: Some Principles, Proposals and Problems', *Evaluation and Research in Education*, **4**, 2.

LOUCKS-HORSLEY, S. and CRANDALL, D.P. (1986) 'Analysing School Improvement Support Systems: A Practical Manual', OECD/CERI/ISIP *Technical Report 3. ACCO* Levier/Amersfort Paris.

MCMAHON, A., BOLAM, R., ABBOTT, R. and HOLLY, P. (1984) *Guidelines for Review and Internal Development in Schools: Primary and Secondary Handbooks*, York, Longman for the Schools' Council.

SCHON, D. (1983) *The Reflective Practitioner: How Professionals Think in Action*, London, Temple Smith.

Part 3

Observation of Classroom Practice

Part 3   Observation of Classroom Practice

A frequent hindrance to the fruitful engagement in the analysis of class-room practice, and of other educational issues, has been the difficulty in reconciling divergent methodological approaches. That these approaches stem from ideological and philosophical perspectives is self-evident.

The three studies in this section investigate the understanding of change in classroom practice. They each have a particular focus and they analyze data which add to the understanding of that area. Bishop and Simpson investigate gender issues in technology problem solving with nursery children and consider appropriate provision and positive classroom strategies. They are also led to consider the methodological implications of participative research. Similarly Thompson and Millward, while bringing insights on children's understanding of poetry in the primary school, discuss the nature of researcher intervention, the effect of working with the class teacher, and the resultant influence on classroom practice. Carneson is concerned to investigate influences on the approach and practice of teachers. This involves the location of micro-study in what is characterized as meso- and macro-analyses of change. The understanding of teacher perspective, and action, becomes layered in rich contexts. This also helps to understand the different perspectives of professionals commenting on classroom practice.

Although an abstract study of methodology is of interest it is essential to recognize the positions and principles underpinning each research approach. It is important to evaluate how the outcomes of a study illuminate the understanding of the issue being reviewed. Research may be methodologically flawed, but this conclusion should be arrived at following an evaluation of outcomes, rather than on a prescriptive view of methodological genesis alone.

Perhaps a useful way of looking at this is by not engaging in a form of normative comparison. The weighing of one methodological approach against another, to judge the worth of the study, is likely to provide an insight into the understandings and prejudices of the reviewer but maybe little else. Rather, if methodologies are seen as non-engaged cogs, some turning quickly, some slowly, some not at all, we may be able to evaluate each on its merits not as a methodology but as providing assistance in understanding the social world. As the size of the cogs is different and the teeth are not always of an inter-locking pattern, each one may need to be looked at on its own merit. The need for disengagement may help to explain why there is a lot of activity but not much progress. A new differential may be required which does not harness the power directly from the process. The energy sources are variable and a sophisticated mechanism is necessary even if the production processes are uneven in terms of efficiency and pollution creation.

The three studies in this section confront methodological issues at the sharp end of investigation. The insights they provide are valuable in their own areas of investigation, but they also allow us to consider the influence of their methodological stance on the outcomes delivered.

7 Problem Solving in Technology in the Nursery: Gender Implications

Alison Bishop and Richard Simpson

The problem of underachievement of girls in physical sciences and technology at the secondary school level and of young women in higher education has been discussed extensively (Kelly, 1981; Whyte, 1986). Recent research (Morgan, 1989; Brown, 1990) would suggest that differentiation according to gender with regard to both attitude and performance in science and technology can be traced back to the primary school. Indeed the National Curriculum documentation for Science states:

> There are some groups of pupils who, according to their teachers and as shown by research, have not, in the past, realised their full potential in science. These groups include girls.

What is more surprising is the statement from the same source that, 'It is likely that the problems of low expectations of many girls particularly in physical science will remain'.

We would argue, however, that such differentiation in respect of both physical science and technology is apparent from the earliest years of education (Bishop and Simpson, 1992), and any attempts to redress it should pay serious attention in the earliest years of schooling. It has been established (Simpson, 1987) that girls aged six years had the perception that both science and technology were 'masculine' activities, and by the age of seven years the identification with masculinity appears to be correlated with physical sciences rather than life sciences (Girdham and Simpson, 1984).

Our own research began with looking at problem solving in technology in the nursery (Bishop and Simpson, 1990). With the arrival of the National Curriculum, technology has become extremely important and is said to be a new subject which, requires pupils to apply knowledge and skills to solve practical problems.

Recent research with regard to design and technology, however, had made little specific reference to activities for children aged 3–5 years. We observed children who were solving a design and technology problem in a number of nursery units. The work reported here is from the third year of the study. Fieldwork was carried out in nursery classes attached to schools in three northern LEAs. Two researchers took part in the investigations, one male, Richard Simpson and one female, Alison Bishop. Detailed observation by us, the researchers, was supplemented by the use of video tape and photographs of activities, plus detailed discussion with both class teachers and nursery nurses. We faced serious methodological problems, not the least of which involved our original decision to enter the nurseries we visited as non-participant observers. The children just would not allow this to happen. Verbal interactions which were ignored were replaced by physical salutations which included arms being flung around legs and our clothing being pulled repeatedly. Richard in particular was seized upon in every nursery we visited and indeed on one repeat visit to a nursery where he did not accompany Alison frequent cries of 'Where is your daddy?', were heard.

We were interested in observing children solving a design and technology problem in units with markedly contrasting patterns of organization. All the nursery units based their organization on exploratory play, some concentrated on a wide experience while others had a highly specific design and technology focus. Some were very much involved in High/Scope strategies in which children were encouraged to formulate their own learning profile, planning their own time allocation over the day. Others followed a more traditional nursery curriculum.

The problem which all the groups were set involved the design and construction of a structure to enable a vehicle to cross a gap between two chairs. A variety of materials was provided to enable to children to design and build a structure. The materials were laid out on a table in the nursery and children were invited to explore the potential of the materials with regard to the set task. On some occasions a group of boys and girls was chosen for us, in other cases the children just arrived through their own curiosity. In all investigations the children were free to enter and leave the group whenever they wished to do so. Because of the difficulties outlined above which we encountered in becoming non-participant observers, we set out the design brief and then stepped back but would, however, speak and interact with a child if a child approached us.

Analysis of video material provided growing evidence of a complex web of gender differentiation occurring within the nursery while technological activities were being implemented. The use of toy cars and lorries, for example, to explain to the children how we needed to cross a gap between two chairs immediately seemed to designate the activity as an activity suitable for boys and not girls. Alternatively, the substitution of a pony or doll made the design task more girl orientated. By the age of three children see toys as gender differentiated and the appeal of the whole technological experience can be weighted towards boys or girls by the materials which are used to present the problem. Thus, if the children were given a choice of a car or a doll when the design task was set, the majority of girls preferred a doll but would accept a car if this was the only tool available. Boys preferred a car and were very reluctant to accept a doll even to the extent of preferring to leave the investigative area to look for a more 'suitable' toy. Furthermore, some children themselves were acutely aware of gender conformity with regard to toys and showed a strong preference for adhering to these rules. Thus when Lego figures were introduced into the technological experience a boy picked up a red Lego figure as part of the problem solving experience. A girl working nearby showed obvious disbelief at this and said to the child, 'There's a blue one'. The boy ignored this and continued working, until the girl picked up the blue Lego figure and put it into the boy's hand whilst removing the red figure for herself with the words, 'That's the boy's toy'. The boy looked at both figures closely and then agreed. It was apparent to the girl, and when pointed out to the boy also, that blue was a boy's colour and red a girl's colour.

It would also appear that, as well as the actual materials which are used to present a design brief, it is also important to consider the area which is used for technological activity. In several nurseries where an area was designated as a construction facility, boys would automatically enter such an area. Even when a mixed group of boys and girls were introduced to this type of designated area the group often became boy dominated. This would suggest that these areas had become boy-owned. In one case, a girl sat on the periphery of such an area, registering interest in the construction activities which had been taken over by boys. When Alison encouraged her to become more actively involved she was able to overcome her initial reticence and she accepted the chance she was offered to explore the materials working alongside the male group. Once Alison moved away from the boys' group, however, the girl stayed only for a few moments before abandoning her task and leaving the area. At no time during this incident did we record any visible pressure of any sort to exclude the girl by the boys although no overtures towards her were recorded.

Where an area of the classroom had not been designated as a construction area and an all boy group had developed, girls would adopt various strategies to take part in the design brief. Some would gain entrance to the group by adopting a passive role, accepting limited space and materials in order to take part in the activity. Others would sit beside the boys and watch patiently (one hour was the maximum recorded for this). Occasionally, a very confident girl would force entry to a group and take part on her own terms. Others would set up a parallel group to work alongside boys. In one incident where a girl and boy were close friends the girl was allowed entry to an all male group because she was with her male friend. The other boys gave the design brief to him and he then passed this on to his female friend. When he left the group the girl left with him and the group then remained male. Similarly, where a group began as an all-girl group, entry for boys was not easy. A frequent strategy recorded by both all-boy and all-girl groups was a refusal to share the design brief with an opposite sex child. Again, reflecting the strategy adopted by the girl to gain entry to the all boy group a boy attempting entry to a girl group managed to gain access to a small area of the work surface using a minimal amount of materials. In this case when Richard approached the group, the boy abandoned the group task saying to him 'Let's you and me have this table'. In most cases both boys and girls would walk into the opposite group for short periods but would then settle back to the single sex group.

In cases where mixed sex groups were deliberately set up children often began tackling the task as individuals. In one nursery, however, a group of three children, one boy and two girls, formed a discussion group to exchange design ideas but remained open to suggestions by visiting children who entered the group. This original group of three remained stable for one and a half hours experience producing a continuous flow of design ideas such that the original construction was continuously refined. Not only did the ideas flow but the structure became more and more sophisticated through cooperation and discussion. It must be stated here that the teacher in charge of this nursery unit was extremely interested in the field of cooperative learning between young children and was very skilled in encouraging conversation between and amongst the children and stressing the need for them to work together as agents of their own learning.

It would appear in fact, that the role of the teacher in setting up and continuing technological investigations for both sexes is crucial. In some nurseries we noted that since the design brief was a technological one some teachers chose a majority of boys to take part. At the most extreme case one teacher commented 'Boys, would you like to build while the girls are washing the dolls?'

In other instances where free choice was given boys were often able to reach the area first which meant it became difficult for girls to enter. As Morgan (1989) states:

> Although the more open style of management is designed to en-
> courage children to develop self-confidence and self-assertiveness
> through the personal choice of activities, this may act against the
> quiet ones, most of whom are girls.

In classes where an area was deemed a construction area it seemed that this area was already in many cases boy owned and any technological activity set up here became a male activity. The re-designation of such areas into a more neutral territory, and the substitution of girl friendly materials, would seem to encourage girl participation.

It appears that gender differentiation exists in a number of varied and quite subtle forms with regard to technological activities in the nursery.

Our research shows that it is possible for boys and girls to work together with regard to problem solving on a technological design brief over an extended period of time. However, such extended cooperation requires a nursery ethos where cooperative working and communication has been fostered and encouraged throughout the nursery curriculum. It is also essential that a careful choice of gender-free resources is made and that the setting in which the activity is based has not already become a boy owned area by a subtle and hidden classroom acceptance that construction activities are for boys.

It is probable that the gender roles adopted by pupils in the nursery are reflecting attitudes acquired in the years before both sexes enter school. If these attitudes are not to become entrenched and indeed reinforced in the school situation then the whole ethos of the nursery becomes a crucial factor in promoting gender equality. Perhaps in order that technological activities do not become closed to girls in the earliest years of schooling we should be considering what positive strategies should be adopted in the classroom. If we are to use conscious intervention techniques to ensure equal access for girls, then we need to consider whether we should be organizing and managing the composition of groups to ensure mixed sex participation or whether we should allocate areas and time throughout the day when girls only are allowed access to technological materials and activities.

References

Bɪsʜᴏᴘ, A. and Sɪᴍᴘsᴏɴ, R.C. (1990) 'Playing with Design and Technology: Experiences in the Nursery', *Education 3–13*, **18**, 3, pp. 36–38.

Bɪsʜᴏᴘ, A. and Sɪᴍᴘsᴏɴ, R.C. (1992) *Gender Differentiation in Design and Technology in the Earliest Years of Schooling*, in preparation.

Bʀᴏᴡɴ, C.A. (1990) 'Girls, boys and technology', *School Science Review*, **71**, 257, June, pp. 33–40.

Gɪʀᴅʜᴀᴍ, A. and Sɪᴍᴘsᴏɴ, R.C. (1984) *Perceptions of young children about science and scientists*, National Conference on Girl Friendly Schooling, Manchester Polytechnic.

Kᴇʟʟʏ, A. (Ed.) (1981) *The Missing Half: Girls and Science Education*, Manchester, Manchester University Press.

Kᴇʟʟʏ, A., Wʜʏᴛᴇ, J. and Sᴍᴀɪʟ, B. (1986) *Girls into Science and Technology*, Department of Sociology, University of Manchester.

Mᴏʀɢᴀɴ, V. (1989) 'Primary Science — gender differences in pupils' responses', *Education 3–13*, **17**, 2, pp. 33–37.

Sɪᴍᴘsᴏɴ, R.C. (1987) 'Science and technology in the primary school', paper contributed to 4th International Conference: *Girls into Science and technology*, University of Michigan Ann Arbor.

Wʜʏᴛᴇ, J.B. (1986) 'Starting Early: Girls and Engineering', *European Journal of Engineering*, **11**, 3, pp. 271–79.

8 Children Talking about Poetry: Changing Classroom Practice Through Teacher Oriented Research

Linda Thompson and Peter Millward

Introduction

This chapter presents the interim report of a pilot study conducted during the summer term of 1990 into children's constructs of poetic genre. It is the research methods, devised and trialled during this pilot project which are the focal point of this chapter. It will be argued that educational researchers can influence classroom practice, not only in established ways, through the dissemination of research findings, but also, at earlier stages of the research project, through the design of research methods which are pedagogically appropriate and which are intended to be used for data collection in classrooms. However, this influence carries responsibilities on the part of researchers; an ethical responsibility to protect young informants and a responsibility to the teaching profession. We will present the range of issues that were considered in designing the research methods for the pilot project.

The pilot project was carried out in two primary schools, one urban, the other rural, in different local education authorities. The research sites were three classes, one infant Y2 class and two junior Y6 Classes. Data were collected from teachers and pupils in a number of ways. In semi-structured interviews teachers talked about their personal understanding and experiences of poetry, together with their philosophy of poetry teaching. These perceptions were incorporated into the analysis and interpretation of the data collected from the children, but will not be presented separately here.

Data from the children was in the form of audio-tape recordings made of their conversations whilst they were engaged in a series of tasks and activities that are presented here as the research method. The data from the Y6 children were complemented by interviews with individual children talking about poems which they had written. These data were collected over a one month period by three researchers who were assuming the role of classroom teachers.

Background to the project: why poetry?

Poetry was selected as an appropriate area of the curriculum for a number of reasons. It has already been identified by other sources as an area of the English curriculum in need of professional consideration. For example, DES (1987, p. 4) commented that poetry was 'frequently neglected and under-resourced, its treatment . . . inadequate and superficial'. While the 1982 DES 'First School Survey' of eighty schools, reported that in the 'majority of schools, poetry was not treated as an important aspect of the curriculum and most children heard it irregularly'. The picture of poetry teaching in junior schools is said to be similar. The '9–13 Middle School Survey' reported that poetry appeared in the classroom 'only as a source material for comprehension exercises and for handwriting practice; for some children the only contact with poetry was through course books' (DES, 1983, p. 52).

In addition, within the National Curriculum, the Programmes of Study (PoS) support the teaching of poetry in relation to the development of a range of language skills. For Speaking and Listening it is suggested that pupils should have experience of: 'reciting poems which they have learnt by heart' (AT 1: Levels 1–3). For Reading (AT 2: Levels 1–3) it is suggested that pupils should:

- hear and share poetry read by the teacher and each other;
- hear poems aloud or on the radio, tape or television;
- take part in shared reading experiences using texts composed and dictated by themselves, as well as, rhymes, poems [and] songs;
- re-tell, re-read or dramatize familiar stories and poems.

The Programme of Study also suggests that pupils would be encouraged to 'play with language', for example by making up jingles, poems, word games, riddles (AT 3: Levels 1–3).

The current situation therefore suggests that there is widespread support, from a variety of influential professional sources, for the teaching of poetry to retain a niche in the English curriculum. However, at the same time there is also evidence to suggest that the situation in classrooms falls short of acceptable practice.

In parallel to the introduction of the ERA there have been other influences on the teaching of English in schools. The Kingman Report (DES, 1988) restated the view that teachers and pupils should have a knowledge of how the English language works in order to ameliorate standards of work in English. This is not altogether a novel view, it can be traced in a variety of documents from the influential Bullock Report, the Cox Report, and more recently, the Language in the National Curriculum (LINC) project. However, the reaffirmation of this view, at the time of impending curriculum innovation on a national level, was a further consideration for teachers of English and was borne in mind when designing the research method.

The research design: overcoming the problems?

Teaching of poetry

It was against this backcloth that the poetry project was designed. Since the project is pedagogically orientated, it was felt important that the design was sensitive to a number of issues of professional concern. First, integral to the research methods devised was an approach to the teaching of poetry which attempted to address some of the perceived shortcomings in the current teaching of poetry in schools. In classroom practice, the teaching of poetry has been characterized by a seeming dichotomy. On the one hand there is the approach which views poetry as a 'marked use of language' characterized by its deviance or anomaly (cf. Levin, 1962). As a theoretical foundation for the teaching of poetry this proves to be deficient and therefore unconvincing for at least three reasons: first, because it is atomistic and does not include a sufficiently comprehensive description of poetry as genre; second, and perhaps more significantly, because it rests upon the pre-supposition of a norm which has yet to be established; and third, it leads to an overemphasis on the mechanistic analysis and comprehension of figurative speech in the poetic form. It is an approach which coincides with earlier behaviourist thinking and its subsequent wider influence on teaching in a number of curriculum areas. This approach is now viewed as a legacy of a mechanistic, somewhat sterile view of language, which is no longer compatible with recent pedagogic developments.

Perhaps in reaction against this approach, teachers began to shift the focus in their teaching to the aesthetic response and appreciation of content. However, this shift did not leave the teaching of poetry without problems, since it thus became linked with one of the concerns central to aesthetic education in general, namely, that 'appreciation' is characteristically understood in both an objective and subjective sense.

While acknowledging this dilemma there is a further concern with the present state of poetry teaching, namely, that the exclusive attention to aesthetic response, is made in the main without rigorous reference to the linguistic form of the genre, identified by Kingman (1988) as a knowledge of how the English language works. The research methods presented here are an attempt to bring together these concerns over the teaching of poetry and to produce a series of activities which offered children aesthetic experience, together with the opportunity to address literary appreciation, while simultaneously including the Kingman call for teaching about how the English language works, specifically in poetic genre. The project was designed therefore to offer an approach to the teaching of poetry which mediates between these existing contrasts.

Learning and teaching

The current state of poetry teaching in school suggests that there is partiality in the existing approaches. Hence it was considered important that the activities designed as the research method represented an attempt to overcome the current situation and present activities that were inherently teaching opportunities and which encompassed the three strands already identified as: literary appreciation, aesthetic response and reference to the linguistic features of the genre.

In addition to fulfilling the primary function of eliciting data from which the researchers could gain insights into the children's developing constructs of poetic genre, the research methods were designed to be teaching and learning opportunities. It was considered important that these activities were concomitant with present primary classroom practice, so they were planned to be in keeping with current classroom culture, as perceived through the eyes of both teachers and learners. It was hoped that the activities were perceived as being engaging, motivating learning activities, which simultaneously provided a high degree of learner autonomy and active participation. This was considered important because it was felt necessary to maintain generally established classroom practice. It was also thought to be desirable that the activities simultaneously taught the children something about poetic genre. The activities were designed to be accepted by teachers as valid, worthwhile learning activities with which the young informants could engage, and to be viewed by the children as familiar learning routines. They were designed to be educationally worthwhile, while also yielding appropriate data. This was considered to be particularly important in the early stage of the research design, prior to refinement, when the research methods were being trialled, and when children were being required to spend substantial periods of time engaged in the activities.

Teacher-Researcher

It was the intention that the data should be gathered in classrooms by researchers in the role of teacher, thereby reducing the possibility of another dilemma frequently faced by classroom researchers as being 'outsiders' to the learning context. It should be stated however, that the adult, (whether in role as parent, teacher, researcher or whatever) will always be an 'outsider' (Milroy, 1980) to the child culture of the classroom. This is not to deny the value of the adult view of the child-world and the child's experience within it, but it is important to note that adults and children will construct differently, even those experiences which they share. The research method presented here is an attempt on the part of the researchers to design a method which is sensitive to the informants who are to provide the data and which is in part autonomous and self-sustained, not requiring the presence of an adult. We hope, therefore, that we have devised inform-ant-centred research methods which are sensitive to the way(s) in which they will be experienced by the children providing the data. Thus, our paramount concern was to design a set of activities which were potentially enjoyable for children and which aimed at including the three dimensions to poetry teaching previously discussed, i.e. the literary appreciation, aesthetic response with simultaneous acknowledgment of the linguistic form. It was felt that the activities should also yield data appropriate to illuminating the research question: what constructs of poetic genre have been formed by children at the ages of 6 and 10 years, and do the children have an appropriate metalanguage for talking about poetry?

These considerations can be presented in summary, diagrammatically:

Figure 8.1   The Research Design: Overcoming the Problems?

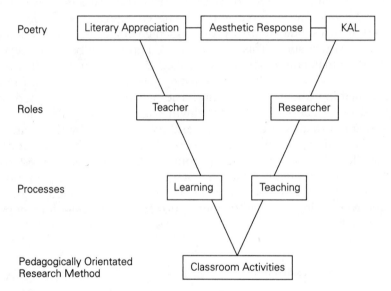

It was in the role of teacher that the researchers collected the data in school classrooms and thereby influenced classroom practice. Whether the influence was positive, negative or at all effective is unsure. However, we hope that it was in no way educationally detrimental to our informants.

A note on ethics

All research carries responsibility. Researchers working in classrooms as-sume an additional set of responsibilities towards the children and teachers from whom they are eliciting their data. The informants are minors, their rights and interests need to be safeguarded. Researchers can respect this in a number of ways: first, by involving parents and school governors when negotiating the research site (this is best negotiated through the headteacher); second, by keeping all parties informed on progress and development throughout the project and finally, by inviting informant-insights on the data collected.

Throughout this project, teachers were regarded as collaborators, actively involved in the research design and trialling of the activities. They also provided informant-insights on data analysis and interpretation. In this way it was hoped to reduce the potential for tension between teachers and researchers and to include legitimate professional concerns into the project design.

The research methods

The research method consisted of a number of activities which were designed to yield data which would illuminate the research questions: what constructs of poetic genre do children have and what metalanguage do they have for talking about their constructs?

Ten activities were designed which, it was hoped would yield appropriate data. The ones presented here are those activities which after trialling and refining were felt to yield the richest data.

Activities 1 and 2: classifying texts

Children were given seven texts and then asked to divide them into two groups, devising their own criteria for the groupings. The texts were selected from a range of children's literature and included, two poems, a letter, extracts from stories, nursery rhymes, a parody of a nursery rhyme and direct speech. The texts were selected because it was felt that they represented a range of literature appropriate for the given age range and included some texts which were possibly already known to the children.

There were two versions of this activity: *Activity 1*, facsimile reproductions of the original texts were intended for use with Y2 children and *Activity 2*, typewritten reproductions of the same texts which adhered to the original layout but which omitted illustrations for use with Y6 children.

No mention of poetry was made by the researchers when presenting this activity to the groups.

Activity 3: selecting texts

Y6 children were given eight poems, typewritten on separate cards. They were asked to select their favourite. The texts included in this activity were selected on the basis of length and the previous responses from child readers. The selection included poems written by living poets, unknown child poets as well as traditional verses.

Activity 10: looking at poetry through poems

This activity consisted of a number of poems about poems. They were selected from an anthology by Morag Styles called, 'You'll Love This Stuff: Poems from many cultures'. It was hoped that this would focus attention on the linguistic form of poetry and hence provide the children with the opportunity to display their knowledge of the genre, using appropriate metalanguage where possible.

These activities were designed to stimulate the pupils' talk about poetry and poetic language. Each activity had two separate stages. In the first stage, the children engaged in peer group discussions about the nature of poetry. The focus at this stage, was on the children's construct of the genre, as articulated in their talk. In the second stage, the children were encouraged to reflect upon their knowledge and use of language and to represent these to the researcher. The activities were designed to encourage a wide range of discourse strategies (discussion, argument, persuasion, agreement, explanation etc.). The discussions were audio-taped. These two stages yielded complementary sets of data. Stage one represented the children's vernacular, more casual speech, while stage two represented a more formal style.

An Interim Report on findings

Categories of development as identified from the data

In the tradition of 'grounded theory' (Glaser and Strauss, 1967), the data collected have been used to identify the following categories of children's developing perception of poetic genre. These categories are not considered to be hierarchical or linear. They do, however, seem to represent a developing awareness of poetic genre.

Poetry as 'given knowledge'

This is evident in a number of statements made by the children when they refer to previous experiences of poetry in the form of nursery rhymes or songs. This initial category we will call 'Given or Common Knowledge'. It is heavily dependent upon previous learning experiences which cannot be identified as specific in time, place or content. Characteristic of this category is the recall of a number of familiar nursery rhymes that represents learning which has taken place but which has been subsequently forgotten. It may or may not have been overtly taught. We consider this to be evidence of Intuitive Knowledge (which is different from an innate predisposition to language learning). The recall of intuitive knowledge is almost second nature. The child can raise this knowledge unconsciously. It is commonplace, effortless recall. In conversation with others, children use a metalanguage (e.g. rhyme, poem, nursery rhyme) as an elliptic referent to their given knowledge and take for granted that their interlocutors share this knowledge. It is frequently presented as a statement of fact:

Example 1:

There is a Miss Muffet so we reckoned that (Little Miss Tucket) might be a nursery rhyme too . . . and we know that's (Sing a Song of Sixpence) a nursery rhyme.

Example 2:

I know . . . they're songs.

Example 3:

And we know that's a letter.

It is the instant, effortless recall which characterizes Given Knowledge as 'Intuitive Knowledge', that is, learning which has taken place but where the circumstances and context of that learning is no longer remembered. In common with all learning it is dependent upon the culture in which it was learned for its meaning and value. It is culture bound and context dependent.

The process of elimination

Developing on from the category of 'Given Knowledge', the informants use their previous learning in their attempt to make sense of the new situation with which they are faced. Through a process of elimination they divide the texts into two sets, those which they *know* to be songs, rhymes, nursery rhymes etc; or those which they consider to share common features with this first group and those which do not. In so doing they also bring to the fore their knowledge and experience of other genres e.g. 'It's not quite a story'. The category is founded on a negative dimension of what the text is not, rather than individual features identified as genre specific.

Example 4:

It doesn't really sound like writing . . . in a way it sounds more like a poem than writing.

Example 5:

It's not quite like a story.

Example 6:

This . . . this . . . this looks like a letter. This sounds like a letter 'cos it says dear, dear Robert. It sounds like it's a letter. It's a letter, so letters are like stories, so they're not poems.

Specific features of poetic form

Two features of poetic structures are the lexis and the syntax. From the data it is apparent that pupils are familiar with the idea of *patterning* in their stylistic description of the genre. The following have been identified by them as distinguishing features of the genre:

(i) The aural quality

Poets usually pattern language to produce specific sound effects and this is frequently recognized by children:

Example 7:

Bits sound like a poem . . . 'The Bishop chanting grace' sounds more like a poem than anything else.

(ii) By association with other genre

When children were unable to articulate identifying features of poetic genre they drew instead upon their knowledge of other genres.

Example 8:

In stories, like, you can write anything; you can write about anything . . . but in poems you have to make it like . . . not just any way, you have to try and make it as though you could say it like a poem.

Example 9:

Because a story is more like writing.

(iii) The form

There are examples from the data of children focusing on the poetic form of a text under discussion and describing the features which classify them as poems.

Example 10:

This rhymes: a pocket full of rye . . . rye and pie. I'll put that in the poem box. Sing and king . . . honey and money . . . blackbird, nose . . . no clothes, nose.

Use of appropriate metalanguage

From the data there is limited evidence to support the view that children have in their linguistic repertoire an appropriate metalanguage for talking about poetic genre. The corpus does however contain some examples of children's use of a metalanguage.

Without an appropriate metalanguage to talk about poetry the children were forced to devise compensatory strategies. These included demonstrating their constructs of the genre with the aid of examples.

Example 11:

If I just read that bit, it tells me that it definitely is a poem.

There is evidence to suggest that children's construct of the genre is more fully developed than their linguistic repertoire for talking about it. This child demonstrates an awareness of the rhythmic qualities of the genre without the benefit of appropriate metalanguage:

Example 12:

A story is like writing. It doesn't even sound like it could get a tune to it, and in other ways a poem does make tunes on it and some of them don't.

The corpus does contain samples of children's use of appropriate metalanguage when talking about poetry but where it does exist it is in reference to the genre (e.g. rhymes, nursery rhymes, poems etc.) rather than in reference to specific features of the genre. Further analysis is required before comment can be made about the details and extent of its existence. However, the metalanguage when demonstrated is not always consistent with its standard use, as demonstrated in this unique contribution.

Example 13:

Oh, is it like doing a teacher as a simile to a puss moth caterpillar

The provisional categories of development suggested here can be summarised diagrammatically:

Figure 8.2   Suggested framework for the development of genre awareness

Category 1   The recognition of familiar texts

Category 2   The recognition of a text as poetry without reference to specific linguistic features

Category 3   The recognition of the genre by reference to specific features without use of metalanguage

Category 4   Inappropriate use of metalanguage

Category 5   Appropriate use of genre specific metalanguage

Tentative interpretations

The Kingman Report (DES, 1988) proposed that teachers and pupils be explicitly taught about how the English language works, its form, structure and meaning as well as its historical and geographical uses. To be able to talk about the language in this way, requires command of the appropriate metalanguage. It is necessary to make a distinction between an individual's ability to recognize specific aspects of language and linguistic form and an ability to talk about them. For the latter, an active command of the appropriate metalanguage is required. However, the lack of the standard metalanguage in an individual's linguistic repertoire, is not necessarily indicative of the absence or lack of awareness of the structure of the language in relation to its meaning. In our data it is clear that in the absence of appropriate metalanguage, children attempt compensatory strategies, to communicate their ideas. Without the appropriate metalanguage to talk about poetry, the children attempt to demonstrate their knowledge of the form and structure of the genre in a number of different ways.

A developing awareness of poetic genre

The evidence to date suggests that there is a developing awareness of poetic genre amongst children as young as six years and that this awareness of specific features is not always accompanied by the standard metalanguage. The data also suggests that there is a range of genre-specific metalanguage in the linguistic repertoire of children aged between six and ten years but that use of the metalanguage does not always necessarily demonstrate an understanding or appreciation of the specific features to which that metalanguage refers.

Observations and insights

There are two directions to the conclusions we draw. The first addresses the roles of the teacher and the researcher. It is our experience that the roles of teachers and researchers do not need to be viewed as entirely separate. Researchers have felt that their influence on classroom practice has been through the dissemination of their research findings. What is suggested here is that if collaboration between researchers and teachers takes place at the planning stages of research projects, research methods more sensitive to the everyday life of classrooms could be devised. Hence researchers would have a more direct impact on classroom activity. The reciprocal understanding between the two groups of professionals engaged in the exercise of improving the quality of learning for children could thereby be enhanced. Through cooperation of this kind, researchers would be able to devise more informant-centred research methods, appropriate to data elicitation from young informants.

The second set of observations is based on insights from the data collected during this project. On the basis of initial analysis we tentatively suggest that children as young as six years are able to demonstrate an intuitive knowledge of poetic genre and are able to distinguish between texts which are poems and those which are not. Further, we would like to suggest that children aged 10 years are able to demonstrate the ability to talk about poetic genre and to display a more developed construct of the genre. However, to date the data suggests that children aged 6 and 10 years have only a partially developed metalanguage in their linguistic repertoire for talking about poetry. A more detailed analysis of the data in the corpus will determine the extent and range of that metalanguage.

We wish to stress that this is a report of the Pilot Project and that the research methods and data analysis presented are provisional. We would therefore welcome comments from interested parties.

Acknowledgments

We should like to express our appreciation to the University of Durham School of Education Research Committee for the financial support which enabled us to buy the recording equipment and expertise necessary during the data collection period of the project. We should also like to express our warm thanks to the teachers and children who gave so generously of their time, energy and expertise and who made the project so enjoyable for us.

References

CARTER, R. (1990) *Knowledge about Language and the Curriculum*, London, Hodder and Stoughton.

DES (1982) *First School Survey*, London, HMSO.

DES (1983) *9–13 Middle School Survey*, London, HMSO.

DES (1987) *Teaching Poetry in Secondary School: An HMI View*, London, HMSO.

DES (1988) *Report of the Committee of Inquiry into the Teaching of English: The Kingman Report*, London, HMSO.

DES (1989) *English For Ages 5–16. The Cox Report*, London, HMSO.

GLASER, B.S. and STRAUSS, A.L. (1967) *The Discovery of Grounded Theory*, London, Weidenfeld and Nicolson.

LEVIN, S. (1962) *Linguistic Structures in Poetry*, The Hague, Mouton.

MILROY, L. (1980) *Social Networks*, Oxford, Basil Blackwell.

STYLES, M. (1987) *You'll Love This Stuff*! Cambridge, CUP.

9   Investigating the Evolution of Classroom Practice

John Carneson

Introduction

Ball and Goodson have argued that in the rapidly changing 'climate of schooling' we need to 'map the teachers' changing perception of their work; the delicate balance between teaching and life' (Ball and Goodson, 1985, p. 24). This chapter presents some of the interim results of a project aimed at developing an approach to the study of change in everyday classroom practice which takes account of this need.[1] Apart from aiming at an ethically viable and methodologically sound approach, the intention was to contribute to the development of a perspective which allows links to be made between three levels of analysis:

— micro-level analyses of a specific teacher's practices;
— meso-level analyses of specific institutions (e.g., a school, an LEA);
— macro-level analyses of those processes which (in a specific society and period) structure the education system.

The main methodological strategy was to link a number of micro-studies, each of which involved tracing observed changes in practice across several data sets. After outlining the research stance and the research design, an account is given of a sample micro-study to illustrate the approach. The chapter concludes by proposing a model for investigating change in individual teacher's practice.

Research stance

The research stance was central to the investigation. It was developed around six principles:

1 The research was aimed at understanding how practice changes and was not directly concerned with improving practice, informing policy or testing specific hypotheses.
2 Methodologically, the research took observed changes in practice as a starting point, rather than pre-specified categories or notions of 'good practice'.
3 In tracing the genesis and evolution of practice the aim was to keep the investigation as flexible as possible. Initial assumptions were kept general, minimal and explicit.
4 Data was contextualized and treated historically so as to avoid superficial comparison or correlations.
5 Practitioners' views, opinions, and experience were treated as significant methodologically and theoretically.
6 The study aimed to be collaborative while recognizing that contradictions and conflicts of interest could not be avoided.

Evolutionary change, at the level of individuals, was initially viewed as being driven by contradictions between what can be described as a practitioner's 'substantial self' (Nias, 1985) on one hand, and elements of educational reality on the other. This implies that the researcher must grasp the world view and concrete situation of individual practitioners in sufficient depth:

a) to enable a meaningful dialogue about change;
and
b) to allow the researcher to locate the practitioner's milieu within institutional (meso) and structural (macro) analyses of change.

Methodology

Andy Hargreaves (1985) suggested a way forward methodologically. Hargreaves argued that for research to be manageable the researcher must select cut-off points in both micro and macro directions. He proposed that middle-range theories could be grounded on 'The growth of linked micro-studies —', as exemplified by his study of middle schools (Hargreaves, 1987) where he linked events in schools to policy decisions at LEA and government level. The basic strategy adopted in the present project was to use discussion with teachers about observed classroom practice as a starting point. Once picked up, the strand of practice was connected with three other data sets: biographical data, data about the institutional contexts, and data about historical factors. Micro-studies were selected on many different tactical grounds, with the intention of eventually weaving them into a series of strategically chosen case studies of change. Micro-studies of particular aspects of change, such as special needs policies or headteachers' change agendas, could be incorporated. Again, the approach was aimed at maximizing flexibility:

a) so underlying processes of change could be uncovered without being threatening to individuals;

and

b) to avoid pre-selecting change factors.

Research design

The core study consisted of three pairs of teachers at an 11–16 comprehensive and two of its (4–11) feeder primaries which are part of a cluster of schools on a complex of estates on the edge of Penmouth, a large Northern town. (Pseudonyms are used throughout). The sample allowed a number of possible lines of enquiry to be pursued. One was size of school: Newdale had about 140 pupils on the roll and Penview, the other primary school, was more than double that size. Both schools are in an area which has had high unemployment since the collapse of the heavy industries the estates were built to serve. Regular visits to classrooms were made during the last term of the 1991–2 school year and the first two terms of the 1992–3 school year, so that issues related to pupil transfer and planning could be followed up. Over a hundred visits were made in this period, including a full week spent in each school. The main sources of data were observation, participative to varying degrees, and interviews and conversations held with various members of staff and key informants who included former teachers, inspectors and advisers.

Sample micro-study of a change in a pattern of practice micro-level data set

Mr. Hayes was a mature entrant to teaching, having worked in retail management for ten years before completing a B.Ed. and then joining the staff at Newdale primary in 1988. The reasons he gave for changing career were boredom with his previous job and liking to work with children, and although he said he had not become a teacher because he 'was desperate to create', it was clear from observations that creativity and innovation played a large part in his practice. Until 1991, when the author began visiting his class, his main experience had been with Year 3 pupils. In the 1991–2 school year, for the first time, two similar 'vertically grouped' classes were formed by mixing roughly equal numbers of Year 4, 5 and 6 pupils. Mr. Hayes taught one and the deputy head, Mr. Palmer (in the next classroom), took the other.

In the first week Mr. Hayes explained that as a temporary measure he was organizing the class into three groups by year as it made planning easier. This strategy, which was quite different from that adopted by Mr. Palmer, became a central feature of a new and highly complex pattern of practice which emerged by mid-term. In order to explore the genesis and evolution of this pattern a number of micro-studies were conducted. In some the unit of analysis was a single lesson: focusing, for example, on the way Mr. Hayes approached dilemmas created by conflicts concerning age, ability and elements of the National Curriculum. (The 'dilemma language' of Berlak and Berlak, 1981, was useful). In others the influence of individual pupils or the impact of changes in the resource environment (e.g., a new computer) was traced over a number of visits. The micro-study reported here concerns the introduction of a carpet which covered a corner of otherwise bare linoleum in Mr Hayes's classroom.

The arrival of the carpet three weeks into the school year prompted Mr. Hayes to experiment with the arrangement of the classroom furniture several times.

Excerpt (i)

Q > I see you've changed the desks around?

T > Yes, moved things around a little, the cupboards [are now in the centre; tops used as a work-surface] it's a bit cluttered now. We might use one to block off the carpet area; it's like this now because we needed to keep it [the carpet] down. But we might keep it this way. (October, 1991)

An example of a further change made in that term was moving the computer off the carpet because the latter encouraged unauthorized pupils to gather around the former. The following were some of the uses to which the carpet was put.

— Once or twice for sitting the whole class down to listen to stories. (This was discontinued for reasons discussed below).
— It was used frequently to sit groups on in order to explain tasks or discuss their work.
— It was used as a work area (e.g. when doing large posters).
— It was used to isolate disruptive children, including those sent from other classes.
— It was used by support teachers working with groups or individuals, or by parents listening to children read.

About three weeks into the second term the old-style desks were replaced by tables of various shapes which could be fitted together in a variety of ways, plus mobile storage units with trays for each pupil. This allowed more space to be created between the year groups and led to a more drastic reorganization of what the author has termed the 'resource environment'. For instance, Mr. Hayes saw an opportunity for advancing his plans to shift from the use of exercise books to storing individual sheets and worksheets in lever-arch files. Following up this kind of clue provided an insight into the way elements both inside and outside the classroom context were interconnected.

> Excerpt (ii)
> T > Just moved things around again, because of the carpet.
> [cabinet off carpet; bookshelves reorganized; one of new round tables on the carpet > T's chair with jacket on it behind it]
> Q > Is that table (on the carpet) there often?
> T > Yes, quite a lot. It's my second desk.
> Q > So the combination of new tables and carpet — sort of work together?
> T > Yes, fantastic. Much more flexible; and there are the storage units. (mobile units with pull-out trays; arrived some time after the tables)
> Q > Are they big enough to get all their things in the trays?
> T > I'm going to put their exercise books in that bookcase; I've also got (lever-arch) files for their work; I've got enough now; but photocopying is going to be a problem. Won't be able to do so much. (because of budget limitations) (July, 1992)

The reference by Mr. Hayes to his 'second desk' in Excerpt (ii) shows how the carpet had become an element in the pedagogical routines he had developed following his decision to organize his teaching according to year groups. As each group worked on a different cycle of topics and tasks he either called them together (often on the carpet) or visited them in situ rather than address the whole class. This was in turn related to two salient trends in his new pattern of practice: a greater stress on independent learning and the less frequent use of project work in favour of relating specific learning tasks to topics and sub-topics. The trends went beyond the general move in the direction of more 'focused' planning attributable to the National Curriculum. Mr. Hayes was aware early on of the impact that teaching three year groups was having on the development of his practice:

> Excerpt (iii)
> I have had to adapt practice a lot; focuses my planning. It is more complicated; have to keep the groups busy — [some eat up the work]. But are they making progress? [refers to three boys]. They'd never get down to work if I didn't push them. Problem is getting them to take responsibility for work — sometimes I feel cruel, telling them to go away — but I have to do it. (end of October, 1991)

Links with the meso-level data set

The close connection between elements in the classroom is well known. Less appreciated are the connections between elements across a school. This is shown by the way a relatively small input of resources (the carpets) could have an impact beyond the classroom as the following example illustrates: Stage blocks which had been nailed down under an old carpet (which was too frayed to cut up) were separated and covered by bits of new carpet. A large stock of all but forgotten but needed exercise books were discovered under the stage blocks, and once the blocks were separated they could be used to good effect in the Christmas play and PE lessons. This kind of change, like minor crises, was perceived as routine, whether in classrooms or at the school level, and thus was more visible to an outside observer than to members of staff. Tracing such change across the school was useful for generating insights into the history and functioning of the institution.

Mrs. Lewis, the headteacher, had been in post since 1990 and had purchased the carpets as part of a refurbishment programme using Local Management of Schools (LMS) funds. As part of her strategy for changing the culture of the school with respect to teacher-management and inter-collegial relations she involved the staff in making decisions about the programme. The staff decided to give individual teachers choice (within guidelines) in the colour of their classrooms, arrangement of notice-boards, shape of tables and so on. This would not have been possible in pre-LMS days when the LEA was directly involved in refurbishing schools and Mr. Hayes twice commented on the speed with which the carpets had arrived.

An LEA adviser reported that carpets were commonly one of the first purchases primary schools made under LMS and this was the case at several neighbouring schools, including Penview Primary. Apart from specific uses, primary advisers and inspectors promoted carpets as 'good practice' as they had a 'civilizing' influence by promoting a friendlier atmosphere and better teacher-pupil relations. For instance, they would recommend that the class sit informally on the carpet for registration, for a discussion, or to listen to a story.

The contrast between the adviser's prescribed use of the carpets (e.g., the whole class on the carpet during discussions, listening to stories or even for registration) and observed use, led the observer to probe general differences in perceptions about discipline and good practice. Mr. Hayes avoided seating the whole class on the carpet, not only because his teaching was group-based, but because he was aware that with those children in that school it might have been counter-productive. The staff, including the headteacher, shared a common understanding of their particular situation: a school in a community with severe social problems. The dominant ethos of the staff was one of 'keeping the lid down' in terms of control, so they could use the resources at their disposal to maximize the life chances of the children by developing them socially and academically. Advisers and teacher-educators from their different positions in the institutional matrix could only partly appreciate this perspective. They were to some extent obliged to abstract good practice from the social context and maintain that a teacher or school need only find the correct strategy to transform a highly disruptive child in the time and conditions available. On the other hand their role and own experience across many schools means they take a panoptic view of individual teacher's or headteacher's change strategies. One adviser said that generally, in her experience, 'The introduction of the National Curriculum — Key Stage One — goes much better if there's collegial cooperation, sense of ownership, including LMS: when there's people party to it'. Similarly, interviews with senior inspectors revealed that they in turn took a broad view of the work of advisers and what drives change in practice.

Some macro-level links

After 1986 the LEA began to rapidly develop advisory and support services, and its INSET programme, and there was heavy investment in a new teachers' centre, but by the time the field-work ended in 1992 various changes in government policy and funding strategies meant that the same areas were being cut back and faced being privatized and fragmented. The relatively new heads who had taken over most of the schools on the estates in the late 1980s were fortunate that they could call on the LEAs for assistance when they most needed it, to use one adviser's phrase, to 'turn their schools round'. The hands of the headteachers in the sample were also strengthened by the implementation of the NC and LMS with the stress on 'whole-school policies'; and a buyer's market for teachers.

One adviser had initial misgivings about LMS but had subsequently seen many instances of 'creative practice involving LMS'. For that adviser the major contradiction between LMS and 'good practice', was that changes in funding ultimately meant dismissing almost the whole support team. There was a complex relationship between the adviser's self-conception as a professional promoting 'good practice'; rapid changes in government policy; and the 'elements' at hand to influence practice on the ground. Senior inspectors, who had some control over semi-macro elements, could take a longer view of a situation in which 'good practice' was one of many factors. The effective introduction of LMS via training courses for school management combined with school-based in-service-training (INSET), set the pattern in terms of the LEA's major input, although the ground was broken by the Technical and Vocational Education Initiative (See Harland, 1987 on the role of funding mechanisms.) More recently, the heads of both primary schools in the study attended a residential course encouraging primary heads to adopt a two-yearly cycle of topics in their curriculum planning and the introduction of appraisal has been similarly managed. In striving to maintain a leadership role the LEA is helping to create a market in which it will have to compete as the government further cuts the functions and resources of LEAs (see Riley, 1992; Davies and Ellison, 1992).

A model of change in classroom practice

Through analyzing the results of a wide range of micro-studies it can be concluded that a holistic view must be taken of teachers' individual decisions. This implies that when Mr. Hayes interacted with pupils, for example, at one or another level he employed perspectives from his professional and biographical experiences, general intellectual interests and religious and political views. This is one way of accounting for the widely noted difficulty in finding causal links between teachers' stated beliefs and specific practices (Zeichner *et al.*, 1987). Over an extended period, however, it was possible to accumulate enough clues to be able to associate clusters of perspectives with particular changes in a teacher's pattern of practice. For example, Mr. Hayes' need to be creative, coupled with his love of history and particular skills, was a strong influence on his curriculum planning. The pedagogy of a secondary teacher in the study was shaped by a conception of science which he formed while working in industry. These kinds of change pressures were termed 'personal', resulting from accountability to self (Shotter, 1984). Two other categories of pressures were discerned: 'public', which was linked to accountability to colleagues, management, pupils and parents; and 'private' which was related to accountability to family, friends, church and so on.

A matrix was formed by introducing the dimension of time (continuous and temporary pressures): for example, getting used to a new class is temporary but meeting the needs of particular pupil would be a relatively permanent pressure. Similarly, Mr. Hayes's first child was born in the course of the study, so awaiting the birth was classed as temporary, raising the child as permanent. A promotion would produce pressures in all the elements in the matrix. The term 'pressure' is not intended to have negative or positive connotations, but investigating perceptions of pressures proved to be very fruitful.

The clusters of perspectives also fell into three categories derived from an analysis of the data: professional, non-professional and general (i.e. orientation to philosophical, ideological and moral systems). The degree to which the various boundaries were permeable, such as private and public; professional and non-professional, became an important part of the analyses, aided by Bernstein's insight into the way boundaries function in maintaining the social order (Bernstein, 1971).

How individual teachers evolve their practice could be understood by investigating what in the model is termed 'framing-control processes'. One reason why teachers have to reframe changed situations is to have more control of elements which are in turn controlling them. The refurbishment of the school changed Mr. Hayes' resource environment and he was able to experiment with those elements under his control. His plans to file children's work (see Excerpt ii) had to be postponed, partly because the extent of his control diminished rapidly beyond his classroom. Photocopying costs had to be kept down and the plan depended on producing lots of worksheets, especially because the school could not afford sufficient sets of textbooks. Because his idea was limited to his classroom (i.e., it was not school policy) he did not ask the school to buy the files and had to accumulate them privately; and so on. The concepts of 'the situation', change pressures, accountability, perspective clusters, reframing and control of elements were brought together diagrammatically in the form of a model (Figure 9.1) from which a provisional typology of change is derived.

Typology of change in classroom practice

Incremental change

The teacher views the change as normal and routine and only partly reframes the situation in the course of making relatively minor adjustments to the basic pattern of practice.

Evolutionary change

Evolutionary change implies a change from one pattern of practice to another which is significantly different. It can be brought about from the progressive effect of incremental changes over a relatively extended period or can happen relatively quickly. The relationship between objective and subjective change, and between action and levels of consciousness, is very complex and varies between individuals and situations. This implies that defining a change as 'significant' must itself be theoretically and empirically justified. The teacher's reframing of a situation may come before, lag behind or be in step with changes in the overall pattern of practice. There appears to be a tendency for teachers to be more conscious of relatively rapid change, but in any case it can be argued that a significant change in the pattern of practice must eventually lead to the teacher reframing the situation.

It should be noted that evolutionary change is a process and a short-term investigation may only reveal incremental change.

Institutional change

The teacher is able, in alliance with others, to effect change in practice by controlling elements beyond the classroom. This usually applies to

Figure 9.1   Model of change in classroom practice

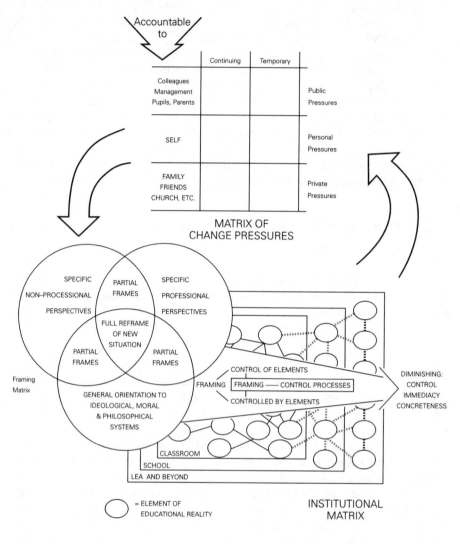

© John Carneson 1993

teachers in the later stages of their careers although the time-frame, degree of intentionality and extent of the change may differ considerably.

Revolutionary change

Socio-cultural boundaries (i.e., between public, private and personal spheres) break down temporarily because of fundamental change in wider society. The author taught in Mozambique shortly after it gained independence. For a while the situation was extremely fluid: hours could be spent probing a teacher's private life in a staff meeting if they were suspected of following the 'old' ways; pupils became teachers and teachers were 're-educated', and in some respects the old formal curriculum became the hidden curriculum (Carneson, 1988).

Conclusion

In this chapter the main concern has been to illustrate how a particular approach was used to study change in classroom practice. The strategy of following a strand of practice in order to accumulate clues across data sets was effective although it gave rise to almost as many ethical problems as fully-participative observation might have done. In particular, there was a tension between investigating classroom practice and exploring micro-political issues, especially in the present climate (cf. Ball, 1987, who rarely discussed classroom practice). On the other hand, the author found that, contrary to Goodson's surmise, teachers often found discussing their practice less threatening than exploring their life-histories (Goodson, 1991). Theoretically, the approach was productive of useful concepts and fresh perspectives on the change process.[2]

The evidence derived from the study agreed in the main with the typology of change as formulated above. However, the evidence also suggests that there are limits to how specific definitions of evolutionary change in teachers' practice can be. For instance, it pointed to the large part played by each teacher's unique configuration of pressures in shaping their practice — not least personal pressures as defined above. The corollary of this is that a more detailed analysis of such change cannot be derived by elaborating abstract theoretical models but must be based on the substantive study of specific changes in particular contexts. This in turn has policy implications as it suggests that universal technocratic 'solutions' to change 'problems' which are based (explicitly or implicitly) on abstract theoretical models will not produce predictable results at the micro-level.

It should be stressed that, while the approach (including the model) contributes to change theory, it was primarily developed to be used as a flexible guide, both for substantive research and for theorizing. Although its main focus is on the individual teacher, it does allow links with meso and macro level analyses to be effectively made.[3]

Notes

1 The project was based at and funded by the University of Sunderland.
2 Concepts and typologies which could not be discussed in this chapter included

areas such as teachers' use of language and the resource environment; and their perceptions of special needs.

3 A recent ethnographic study of policy implementation (Bowe *et al.*, 1992) unfortunately made few references to changes in everyday classroom practice.

References

BALL, S. and GOODSON, I. (1985) 'Understanding Teachers: Concepts and Contexts', in BALL, S. and GOODSON, I. (Eds.) *Teachers' Lives and Careers*, London, Falmer, pp. 1–26.

BALL, S. (1987) *The Micro-Politics of the School*, London, Routledge and Kegan Paul.

BERLAK, A. and BERLAK, H. (1981) *Dilemmas of Schooling*, London, Methuen.

BERNSTEIN, B. (1971) 'On the classification and framing of educational knowledge', in YOUNG, M.F.D. (Ed.) *Knowledge and Control*, London, Collier-Macmillan.

BOWE, R., BALL, S. and GOLD, A. (1992) *Reforming Education and Changing Schools: Case Studies in policy sociology*, London, Routledge and Kegan Paul.

CARNESON, J. (1988) *Towards a theoretical understanding of revolutionary curriculum change*, M.A. dissertation, Institute of Education, London.

DAVIES, B. and ELLISON, L. (1992) 'Delegated school finance in the English educational system: An era of radical change', *Journal of Educational Administration*, **30**, 1, pp. 70–80.

GOODSON, I. (1991) 'Sponsoring the teacher's voice: Teachers' lives and teacher development', *Cambridge Journal of Education*, **21**, 1.

HARGREAVES, A. (1985) 'The Micro-Macro Problem in the Sociology of Education', in BURGESS, R., *Issues in Educational Research: Qualitative Methods*, London, Falmer.

HARGREAVES, A. (1987) 'Past, Imperfect, Tense: Reflections on an Ethnographic and Historical Study of Middle Schools', in WALFORD, G. (Ed.) *Doing Sociology of Education*, London, Falmer, pp. 17–44.

HARLAND, J. (1987) 'The New INSET: a Transformation Scene', in MURPHY, R. and TORRANCE, H. (Eds.) *Evaluating Education: issues and methods*, pp. 123–34, London, Harper, pp. 123–34.

NIAS, J. (1985) 'Reference Groups in Primary Teaching: Talking, Listening and Identity', in BALL, S. and GOODSON, I. (Eds.) *Teachers' Lives and Careers*, London, Falmer, pp. 105–19.

RILEY, K. (1992) 'The changing framework and purposes of education authorities', *Research papers in Education*, **7**, 1, March, pp. 3–25.

SHOTTER, J. (1984) *Social Accountability and Selfhood*, Oxford, Basil Blackwell.

ZEICHNER, K.M., TABACHNICK, R. and DENSMORE, K. (1987) 'Individual, Institutional and Cultural Influences on the Development of Teacher's Craft Knowledge', in CALDERHEAD, J. (Ed.) *Exploring Teachers' Thinking*, London, Cassell, pp. 21–59.

Part 4

Teachers and the Impact of Professional and Organizational Development

Part 4   Teachers and the Impact of Professional and Organizational Development

In the last section teachers are the centre of attention. Here the focus is on how teachers 'make it happen' and how they think about their work. The authors detail courses and projects designed to improve practice. This section presents research which attempts to connect outcomes with understanding change, and to contribute to the improvement of support for teachers in improving classroom practice. The chapters combine efforts to chart the impact of professional and organizational development with understanding how change takes place.

Dadds argues that award bearing courses facilitate meaningful change in classrooms and for schools. However the assessment systems for such courses have an awkward place in this process, sometimes adding to the process and sometimes not. Her argument suggests that the problem lies rather deeper than revisions in the form of assignments will cure and is to be found perhaps in a deeper understanding of the different ways in which teacher thinking and change can support each other.

Norton has traced the effect in schools of an LEA-led initiative specifically aimed at the renewal of primary classroom practice. He has made an analysis of the effect of the initiative on teachers' professional lives. He argues that observed changes are of limited worth in capturing an understanding and instead draws on biography as a way of understanding the importance of the personal in teachers' practice. Through this he is able to draw out the teachers' perceptions of the new orthodoxy, and the sense they make of pressures to change.

Vulliamy and Webb followed up teachers after a long award-bearing INSET course. They consider the relationship of the course to change in practice. What emerges from their work is the importance of the context of change. Teachers also pointed out their increasing realization of listening to and understanding the concerns of colleagues, and reflection upon data gathered in the work situation. Vulliamy and Webb note that the emphasis on organizational as opposed to classroom change found in work on school improvement may not be helpful.

A further major effect noted by Vulliamy and Webb was in the teachers' attitudes to pupils. Teachers' professional lives are of course focused on pupils, so at first sight this may not be a result to make readers sit up and take notice. However this finding deserves pondering upon. Work on change suggests that disproportionately too much time is spent on planning and the initiation of projects, whereas little attention is given to implementation and institutionalization of change. In other words, last year's innovation isn't news any more, and yet, teachers' central concern — pupils — remains throughout their career. It is perhaps surprising that the importance of the renewal and refreshment of teachers' engagement with pupils goes so little remarked upon. Therefore an example such as this of a means by which teachers' attention to their central professional concern, pupils, may be renewed (again and again and again?) is of paramount importance.

The idea of pupils as one among many audiences for teachers is evident in this section. Teachers find themselves in a context with pupils as but also with other and more powerful audiences and contexts. In all three chapters the tensions for teachers between their audience of pupils and other audiences is present.

10 Can INSET Essays Change the World for Children?

Marion Dadds

Tears balanced on the edges of Annie's eyes as she faced me in supervision. Her Advanced Diploma research essay had not been finished and the submission date was a cat's whisker away. As her course tutor, I had mixed feelings about her predicament. 'But who am I supposed to be writing this for?' she challenged me. I was sure this question was not rhetorical, and unsure about whether Annie had a view of how I should answer. It was more of an accusation than an invitation to rational discourse. But she had distress on her side and I needed to be careful.

My immediate and somewhat impulsive hypothesis was a simple one. Annie had not written the essay because she was a procrastinator *par excellence* who was fearful of the commitment which the written word demanded. But my impulse was tempered by some empathy. I knew that although Annie was a strong critic of the award-bearing system each time essay submission date hovered, she was also devoted to the cause of classroom improvement through her own professional development. She was keen to put her research-based Advanced Diploma course to sound practical use for her pupils. Simple though my immediate hypothesis was, I felt uncomfortable with the uncomplicated colour in which I was trying to paint her failure to submit on time. 'Who then?' I asked her.

This was her cue to stimulate my guilt for being the award bearing tutor and examiner, and for making these unreasonable and not too helpful literary assessment demands on her. In payment for her own stress and uncertainty, she offered me the chance of some self-remorse for requiring her to commit her action research project to permanent textual written account. The tears retreated from the edges of her eyes. 'But I have done research. You know I have. What difference is the essay going to make to the children? It's only for the award in the end.'

She proceeded to remind me of the breadth and scope of her small scale enquiry into the design and development of a new and vastly improved play area in her primary school. She reminded me of the numerous ways in which the children had been involved; how the ideas from parents and governors had been canvassed; how the children had invited the county recreation officer into the school to give help and advice; how they had started trying to raise funds from local sources. The children had designed prototypes and drawn up scale plans and models. They had considered safety, cost, variety, equal opportunities, play needs and preferences of children from four to eleven years old.

> 'If this is supposed to be action research, isn't all this action good enough?' she challenged. 'You've seen the practical impact the project has had from your own visit to the school.'

I could deny Annie none of this. There had been widespread, purposeful and communal action in the process of doing this small scale action research project. Her third and fourth year junior class had become researchers themselves, interviewing parents, teachers and fellow pupils. There had been consciousness-raising of children, staff and parents in the processes of fieldwork, in the use of the data gathering methods, in the many discussions which had been generated by questions Annie had asked about play provision. Annie had organized and chaired several staff meetings in which she had shared data and insights from the research with colleagues. The staff meetings had been the means by which corporate decisions of principle had been taken on the need for radical improvement. Annie had persuaded colleagues to accept that maximum involvement by the children could also generate worthwhile educational experiences as well as offering well-founded radical proposals. The children had mounted a display of the work which had grown from the project. Children had talked to interested parents about the display after school.

I had to admit to my delight and regard for all that had been achieved so far. What had been a drab and boy-dominated tarmac area alongside an open field would be transformed as a result of Annie's project. Years of recreational habit and assumption at the school had been interrogated by her research and had been found wanting. A more creative, divergent and community-sensitive alternative is evolving. 'So isn't this good enough as action research, then after all that has happened?' Annie repeated. 'And will continue to happen', she added just for good measure.

Silently, I thought, 'Not until it is made public', though I kept this little pomposity to myself, for I had no wish to risk the rush of the tears again. 'Research is systematic enquiry made public', I chanted secretly to myself, like some inner incantation, remembering the sentiments of the late Lawrence Stenhouse. Dave Ebbutt's words also passed across my mind — his belief that teacher's small scale enquiries should be committed to print for the public good if they were to gain a place and status in the world of research. 'If action research is to be considered legitimately as research,' he had written, 'the participants in it must, it seems to me, be prepared to produce written reports of their activities' (Ebbutt, 1983, cited Hopkins, 1985, p. 118). Moreover, he had argued that 'these reports ought to be available to some form of public critique' (p. 118). And in my heart I could not disagree with Ebbutt's position when he said, 'I would go so far as to say that if this condition is not satisfied then . . . it is not action research' (p. 118). How else would other professionals validate, or benefit from, teacher action research if it were not to be made public in this way?

Yet these stringent conditions seemed harsh, even to a convert like me, in the face of the professional energy which Annie had invested in the project. Tears and the labour of writing seemed a perverse kind of reward for such professional goodwill, commitment and generosity of spirit, and for thorough enquiry, sensitively and communally conducted. Were we, in academia, in danger of creating the 'invisible college' of which Walker (1985) once spoke? He wrote of the historical and scientific expectation that research should be primarily communicated to the scientific peer group (p. 118). It is this 'invisible college,' he argued, that scrutinizes and legitimizes research, and that perpetuates conventional views of what constitutes an appropriate research text. Annie might well have argued, had I risked entering this minefield, that her work had not been primarily directed towards the wider research community or the invisible college. As such, the textual demands of the invisible college were, to her, inappropriate.

'You know I am only writing it for you, after all this, you and the examiner. It is not for me or the children. I just want you to know that. Who on earth will have time to read it in school, anyway?'

In my heart I knew this to be the case — for Annie, for students past and for many more still to come. It was not always because of colleagues' lack of willingness that Advanced Diploma research reports failed to be read in school, though this was sometimes the case. It was often more to do with the busy, demanding shape and style of life in school that denied the effort to sit down individually or collectively and read four thousand or eight thousand or twelve thousand award-seeking words.

Annie's spirit took an upturn, having externalized these recurrent literary anxieties. Yet we both knew, but did not say, that the research report had to be written if Annie wanted her Advanced Diploma. Those were the regulations. She closed her data file, packed full of questionnaires, interviews, notes, photographs. She pushed it deep into her National Trust bag, alongside a clutch of children's green exercise books, and rose resignedly from the supervision chair. An open hand was raised in gesture of peace, recognition and farewell.

Off she went, knowing she would have to bind herself to the pain and trouble of writing. For my part, I reassured myself that this commitment to written words was a commitment to meaning-making, a process of thought construction itself, a possibility of self-transcendence (Winter, 1989). It would do Annie good. It would clarify thought for her. It would compel her to organize ideas and material which were currently disparate and atomized. It would produce linguistic coherence where little previously existed. So I thought. So I rationalized.

But much that she had said continued, inevitably, to haunt me. I still had no doubt that fear and distaste of writing were parts of Annie's problems, as they were with very many students. But her critique prevented me from settling to my usual complacent certainty about the educative value of the writing process for hard-pressed, award-seeking teacher action researchers. Their time and energies were finite and they were as keen as anyone to use them as wisely as possible in order to improve the world for young children. Annie had conducted her enquiry. It had fostered multiple beneficial educational change and would continue to do so. How would the written research report add to any of that? And how many members of the invisible college would ever read it?

Annie's feelings and experience have been reflected in those of countless other students before and after. Many do not see value in writing about the fruits of their research, not even to satisfy the regulations of an award undertaken voluntarily. As such, Annie's critique raises important questions for award-bearing teacher action research which cannot be ignored. In the first place, Annie's challenging question about writing for an appropriate audience was a valid and central one, and it showed that for some award-seeking teacher researchers there is a tension and contradiction in the textual requirements of their courses. Who are they writing for? Are their research reports for themselves, for their school communities, for the course examiners, for a wider and anonymous professional peer readership?

Research-based INSET claims to be orientated towards the cause of classroom improvement through the professional development of teachers, yet Annie felt that the award-seeking text was orientated towards the examiners as audience, not towards the professional audiences within her school, nor even towards her own professional developmental needs. It was, simply, a task and a text she had to get though in order to satisfy awarding criteria. It was not work that she felt added to the practical and reflective developments which had already taken place. Nor can the issue of audience for the text be divorced from the question about purpose for the action research. Annie was quite clear that her research essay was to be written solely for the purpose of assessment. It was not serving the prime purpose of aiding practical development of action within her school. The finding out, the reflection, the analysis and much of the significant action had already happened before pen was shown to paper (or not shown to paper, in Annie's case). So, to what practical effect were her subsequent literary endeavours spent? The question was a genuine vexation for Annie and became a vexation for me as her INSET tutor and examiner. If it was an accounting for the purpose of accreditation, could the effort not be spent more wisely for school improvement by students such as Annie whose communication skills and strengths lay in directions other than the traditional written text? That Annie had, nevertheless, communicated aspects of the research to school audiences without writing her traditional Advanced Diploma essay is relevant, for it suggests that action-orientated texts for practical, action-orientated school audiences may be more effective if developed in modes other than the more standard research essay or report.

Some of Annie's INSET colleagues have had different experiences of writing. Text creation had undeniably served a purpose of cognitive organization, clarification and development of ideas. These cognitive processes may have been essential to the creation of insights. As such, they may have been precursors to any judgments made about further practical action. This was not so for Annie. For her, judgments about practical ways forward in her project, and decisions about action steps from research findings, were created in the doing of the project, not in the creation of a written research text. Annie's was a classic example of what Schon (1983) has termed reflection in action, or what Elliott (1981) called a practical theory. Elliott (1981) suggested that 'In action research, theories are not validated independently and then applied to practice, they are validated through practice' (p. 1). For Annie, insight, theory and action from her research enquiry were all generated through the many other processes involved in doing the research, not through the composition or presentation of the formal written award-seeking text. The text in that sense made no contribution to the action research, nor to developments in the practical world of the children. It was, simply, an activity of summative reporting and description, for an audience she neither chose or knew, and that had no investment in the project.

Many standard written research texts do, indeed, embody theoretical insights and hold the potential for adding to professional educational knowledge. As such, they may have a potential contribution to make to the thought that precedes change. But they will only make that contribution if other potential users read them. Texts that are not presented in forms which interested colleagues are able to access effectively carry dead professional knowledge and educational dust. They certainly will not, as such, be action orientated texts and may fail to become catalysts for improvement and development.

Holly (1984) once asked of the academic-bearing world, 'Whose needs are we serving?' He argued that the award-bearing culture of academia may have timetables, deadlines and regulations for teacher action researchers that do little to help them to use their research for anything but an individualistic, award-seeking purpose. I would also argue that the traditional written research report may be convenient mainly for the award-giving institution and the examiners. It may fit comfortably into the academic culture with its normative textual approaches to communicating knowledge. The students are socialized into certain normative academic conventions — standard construction of bibliographies; presentation of data in supplementary appendices for validating the internal nature of the research; in some cases, standardized bindings and lettering (the higher the award, the more standard becomes the binding); citation of relevant authorities. It is easy to see the sense and wisdom of some of these conventions where texts are designed to communicate to a distant and impersonalized audience. Yet it is also easy to see that creating texts to these norms for the purpose of seeking an award will involve the student in an academic learning that may contribute little, if anything, to developments in schools or classrooms. And these may not be the kinds of texts that more naturally fit the reflective and practical purposes of the school culture. Tight bibliographies, standard referencing and double spaced black bound texts may not be perceived as practically helpful by teachers even though they serve the conventions of the award-seeking purpose.

One could argue that the learning process for the teacher in an award-bearing context is the process of re-socialization or acculturation. In this process they are required to cross the bridge from their school-based professional culture into the more academically orientated culture of the awarding institution. This requires transformation of the teachers' way of thinking, speaking, writing, for the discourses of the dominant academic culture, and the manner of conducting those discourses may not necessarily match the discourses of the school (Gore, 1989a, 1989b). Thus, validation and awarding may be seen as a process of cultural reproduction in which the dominant culture maintains its power base. This is ironic given that school-based practitioner research was seen to be a better and more appropriate alternative than accessible traditional educational research (Stenhouse, 1975), for if the fruits of teacher action research cannot be used by the Annie's of the award-bearing world because of the forms in which they are communicated, we have made very little progress.

The problem, of course, is not just an aversion to writing, nor of textual credibility, but may also be one of time. It may be that Annie's painfully created texts did have potential credibility for colleagues because they were the texts of someone that school colleagues knew and trusted. Also, school colleagues had an identity and, thus, a potential interest in the studies. Yet in their award-bearing form, these texts had no operational external validity because school colleagues could not find time to access the wisdom in them effectively. As such, the knowledge from the research could have been dead professional knowledge with no practical applicability. External validity only became operational when Annie communicated the findings from her enquiry in ways that emerged naturally from the working and culture of the school. These alternative forms of communication were manifest through the consultative and expository staff meetings, through the displays of the children's related work, and through the actual practical developments which could be seen and discussed by all.

On the other hand, Annie's course colleague, Vicki, made much practical school-orientated use of the text she created from her major research study on the course. This study looked at gender practices in a range of situations in her school, setting the findings against a wide review of literature, theory and other research. The final written text amounted to some fifteen thousand words and drew upon interviews, questionnaires, observations, photographs and various documents.

School interest in the study was high. Vicki was invited to lead a staff development day on the work with a view to guiding colleagues towards the beginnings of an equal opportunities policy. Vicki became an INSET agent overnight. The insights and material from her major research study became the substance of the INSET and the stimulus for school colleagues' professional development. Having created a research text which satisfied the award requirements and which fed her own professional development, she now sought to transform that text into new modes of communication for a new purpose and a different audience. The resulting staff development event involved all her school colleagues. In leading this, Vicki relied predominantly on oral rather than written forms of communication as Annie had done when chairing staff meetings. Vicki explained to colleagues the main findings of the study in an oral presentation; she structured group discussions using material from her research text; she generated debate and drew colleagues' responses together in a set of suggestions for ways forward on the school equal opportunities policy.

In this, we see Vicki using her 'situational understanding' (Elliott, 1991, p. 122) to make judgments about the most appropriate form of 'text' to suit her colleagues' INSET purposes. Her fifteen thousand word, neatly bound, Advanced Diploma long study had cut little ice with her busy colleagues' schedules, even though colleagues were keen to relate to the Pandora's box of insights between the binding. 'She's invited us to read her study, but she hasn't stuffed it down our throats,' one of her colleagues had told me. And time proved that the multifaced 'text' of the INSET event, encoded predominantly in spoken communication, was much more effective in sharing developing areas from Vicki's research than the more time-consuming written text.

But the demands on teacher action researchers of creating these trans-formed or alternative texts should not be underestimated. Vicki invested much time, effort and thought in preparing materials before the day, and for the day. Also, she had to find new levels of self-confidence and skill as a professional communicator for a venture she had not previously encountered. 'Well, I was nervous,' she told me 'But it was just that when I started to talk, it didn't flow to begin with and I was tripping over my words and all the rest of it. You know, my colour rose.'

Her colleagues were encouraging, supportive, kind, for they respected Vicki. They wanted her to draw from the substantial learning she has undertaken and do well. They appreciated the style, length and content of the input she had prepared. 'Vicki gave a presentation first,' Antony explained, 'which I think was suitably short. It didn't try and explore the whole scene,' he continued, 'but it dipped into some of the issues which we might consider.'

For discussing the many related issues of equal opportunities, Vicki organized her colleagues into small groups. The wisdom of this was appreciated for it allowed a much more conductive context than the full staff group for the lengthy, complex and often personalized gender discussions that followed. But Vicki discouraged abstract discussions evolving that failed to relate back to practical developments in school. She injected practical challenge into the work and she encouraged a strong link between ideas and action.

'When she set us the target of evolving a school policy,' one colleague recalled, 'She . . . said, I don't want sort of grand phrases, I want identifiable nitty-gritty things that you think could be changed in school.'

The debate about the issues was forthcoming and the suggestions for practical action followed hot on its heels. These ranged, according to Antony, 'right from . . . the formalized structuring of the policy of the school, right down to everyday issues of how we approach each other and children in the staff and classroom.'

Reflections generated by the day carried over into colleagues' daily work; into their selection of literature for pupils; into their awareness of the use of computers; the presentation of role models in technology, domestic subjects, history; the gender balance of the staff group itself; the gendered use of language. The issues and practical suggestions for a first draft policy were drawn together by Vicki and the deputy head.

Twelve months after the event, colleagues gave testimony to the continuing awareness of, and sensitivity to, gender issues in their daily work. The impact of Vicki's research and its transformation into the school-based INSET event had stayed with people. For many, the personal change had become irreversible. For this to be achieved by a blushing, nervous, but determined teacher action researcher with no previous experience as an INSET agent was no mean achievement. It was quite unlikely that anything on this scale could have been achieved by the use of her written award-bearing text alone.

Annie and Vicki thus developed their own alternative forms of communication for school audiences. In this, they demonstrated that it may, indeed, be neither possible nor desirable to reconcile different purposes and the needs of different audiences in the one, single, award-seeking text. They also demonstrated that award-bearing research-based INSET can, indeed, serve the needs of colleagues, children and practical school improvement — providing that the award-seeking researcher is prepared to invest much extra effort, wisdom, time, skill and hard work beyond that required to write their essays and long studies for their award.

These transformed texts which we could see as 'enactive' texts in the

Brunerian sense, required as much skill, judgment and wisdom of the teacher action researchers as the creation of their standard written research texts. Indeed, more was required of an interpersonal nature, for these 'enactive' texts of Vicki's INSET event and Annie's school-based activities involved an interpersonal understanding and sensitivity that the written text did not. Vicki and Annie were using their research to stimulate and support the professional understanding and development of colleagues. In this, much more professional learning than their own was at stake. And, in both cases, much more was gained through the spoken, enactive INSET discourses than through the written. Yet these transformed modes of communication for school audiences, the modes that generated the practical action from the enquiry, were not accredited.

It is my contention, and conviction, that these alternative, enactive, school-orientated 'texts' are as worthy of an award as the written texts from which they are transformed or which, in Annie's case, they precede. For they constitute in themselves award-worthy work of a substantial nature. They also help to change the world of schooling for children.

There may be other alternative action-orientated texts that the award-bearing world can help teachers to develop, that are a more integral and natural part of the school culture and that have a greater chance of fostering worthwhile change. Rob Walker pointed out that this may be an under-developed part of the action research enterprise. He wrote, 'Finding effective means of communication in applied research studies is an area that is undeveloped in reaction to the effort that has gone into devising methods and techniques for data collection.' (Walker, 1985, p. 164)

Tentative beginnings to explore such alternatives were made on the course following Annie's and Vicki's. Students were offered the opportunity to create non-traditional texts for their assessed work. The texts could, if the student chose, be orientated towards school audiences and towards practical school and classroom developments. The texts would, nevertheless, be constructed upon insight, hypotheses and theories generated from small scale systematic enquiry or from critical reading, or from a combination of both these reflective starting points.

Alternative texts were suggested. These included staff and curriculum discussion documents; draft policy documents; staff development and INSET material such as video or tape-slide sequences; material or documents for use with parents or children. Students were also encouraged to develop other texts that they judged might be well matched to purposes and audiences of their choosing. Enactive texts of the kind that Vicki and Annie had spontaneously created for their colleagues were included in these alternatives. On the other hand, students were not discouraged from writing solely for themselves, nor from clarifying their own understanding through the writing process, using a more traditional research essay or report format. All of these choices were made available and students were encouraged to match choice to their own purposes. Not all students were in school contexts that encouraged, enabled or supported sharing and dissemination from individual INSET. Similarly, some students wanted and needed to use their Advanced Diploma enquiries for their own individual professional development, and school audiences were not their priority. These individual differences in need and school context meant that variety and choice had to be available.

There was no invisible college in my own institution preventing innovation. On the contrary, several colleagues expressed much support and curiosity. Formal institutional approval was given readily. The first stage of this innovation is awaiting evaluation. Meanwhile, the question is still with me. Are we sure that our traditional award-seeking action research texts are not standing in the way of practical school improvements? There also remains the need to question our own academically-orientated assumptions and to test our school improvement rhetoric against our academically-orientated practices.

Of the innovation, students were enthusiastic, though it transpired that in resolving some old problems, we created some new ones. But that's another story.

References

EBBUTT, D. (1983) 'Educational action research: some general concerns and specific quibbles', Cambridge Institute of Education, Mimeo.

ELLIOTT, J. (1981) 'Action research: A framework for self-evaluation in schools', Cambridge Institute of Education.

ELLIOTT, J. (1991) *Action Research for Educational Change*, Milton Keynes, OUP.

GORE, J. (1989a) 'The struggle for pedagogies: Critical and feminist discourses as regimes of truth', paper presented at the eleventh conference on Curriculum Theory and Classroom Practice, Ohio, October.

GORE, J. (1989b) 'Discourses of teacher empowerment: A post-structural critique', paper presented at AARE conference, Adelaide, November — December 1989.

HOLLY, P.J. (1984) 'Beyond the cult of the individual: Putting the partnership into in-service collaboration', in NIAS, J. (Ed.) *Teaching Enquiry Based Courses*, Cambridge Institute of Education.

HOPKINS, D. (1985) *A Teacher's Guide to Classroom Research*, Milton Keynes, OUP.

SCHON, D. (1983) *The Reflective Practitioner*, New York, Basic Books.

STENHOUSE, L. (1975) *An Introduction to Curriculum Research and Development*, London, Heinemann.

WALKER, R. (1985) *Doing Research: A Handbook for Teachers*, London, Methuen.

WINTER, R. (1989) *Learning from Experience: Principles and Practice in Action Research*, Lewes, Falmer.

11 Primary Teachers Experiencing Change

Jerry Norton

Change in classroom practice is a multi-dimensional process in which the substance of change can sometimes be seen as being synonymous with changes in observed actions and organization. Observed changes are valuable, but in themselves may be of limited worth in the understanding of change. Perhaps, to gain a deeper understanding of the teaching process and how it changes, there is also the need to understand how the practitioner makes sense of the process and how the influences that generate change are accommodated within the teacher's own beliefs and actions. The importance of biography, in this process, has been realized and valuable investigations are helping to develop an understanding of the relevance of the personal, in the practice of the teacher.

This chapter results from a study of primary schools involved in a LEA-led policy initiative. The initiative had a number of aims but central to the programme was a rejuvenation of classroom practice. An attempt is made to explore some of the issues which influenced policy formation and implementation, and how it affected teachers in one school. From the study, which extended over four years, aspects of early conversations with four teachers are used to illustrate the impact of the programme on their professional lives.

The generation of a new orthodoxy

It is possible to make sense of part of the context in which practice operates by examining views of how initiation into the teaching/learning process takes place. Tomlinson (1990) has suggested there has been a move away from technical rationality (Schon, 1983), (the understanding of education through theories, concepts and ideas, which the teacher is asked to apply in the classroom), to technical procedurality (Tomlinson, 1990), (in which the emphasis is on doing and learning through action), and this may have encouraged a reductionist new orthodoxy. The discipline based approach to teacher education and professional development may not have been replaced with an adequate framework for those primary teachers trained within the technical rational framework. Some of this group of teachers became successful, reaching positions of influence, in the post-Plowden era. The weight of managerial responsibilities in a hierarchical structure, (Winkley, 1985) when coupled with inadequate initial training and professional development (Alexander, 1984), appears to have left many headteachers and advisers with an engagingly anti-intellectual approach to teachers as thinkers and innovators. This attitude to theorizing was, at least in part, a result of the failure of technical rationality to inform classroom practice, and the later adoption of a technical proceduralism which has often centred on child-centred coping strategies.

As the academic base of teacher education proved unhelpful in the everyday world of the classroom, teachers became, if they were not already, disillusioned with theory. This does not seem promising for those who wish to promote new forms of pedagogy. If teaching is seen by the practitioners as a largely pragmatic exercise, in which the questions of what is done and how it is done are seen as unproblematic, it may be difficult to develop a new orthodoxy. However, the adoption of a procedural, reductionist model which has wide-spread currency amongst powerful actors in an LEA can pose a clear and unproblematic way forward. A consequence of this is that teachers will be encouraged to think about problems of implementation, but not about the underlying theory.

Perhaps as part of this account we should consider the priorities of teachers (Goodson, 1991) and the influence their own priorities have on action and attitude (disposition). This may take us further than the observation of behaviours, into the realm of reactions and intentions. Resistance, adoption, or adaptation to change can therefore be analyzed through the attitude of the practitioner to the ideology, strength and direction of change. This is further complicated by dissociation between what is said and what is done by teachers (Reynolds and Saunders, 1987) and by what Hargreaves (1992) suggests is the need to change teachers as people.

As has been suggested, teachers are faced by changing definitions of what good practice is; this may be viewed as the social construction of quality in teaching (Lawn, 1991). Many of those teachers involved in the programme had been trained in the era of technical rationality and yet, were being asked to operate a form of practice which was dominated by a procedural approach. As has been implied, the new espoused practice was loudly championed by many who had achieved positions of influence, as advisers and headteachers. However, it was also taken up by two other groups. The first group realized that career advancement lay through support and implementation of the programme. The second identifiable group were those young teachers whose training had been highly influenced by the technical procedural approach and welcomed the challenge, to what they saw, as unambitious and limited practice.

The investigation

By examining the background and experiences of four teachers, in one school, an attempt is made to explore some of the complexities of the impact of the programme on the individual (this is a sub-sample of a larger group of teachers regularly seen over a period of nearly four years). In doing this it should be noted that the implementation of the programme was phased and uneven in its impact. The interviewing procedure became increasingly less structured over time. This was due to a shift in focus toward the biographic, an increasing lack of certainty as to the major influences on practice and also to the use of conversation as research discourse.

The concern is centred on how teachers are affected and influenced by an externally sponsored initiative. The question of external influence has already been touched on. The complexity of this relationship cannot be explained by a rational view of decision making and implementation. The gap between that management and organizational theory, which ideally represents the process of institutional functioning and the realities of the problematized world of the school, have been thoroughly explored elsewhere. As Goodson and others have made clear, resistance to change and a dominant ideology is complex, especially as a false accommodation can be achieved because of differences in rhetoric and reality. We may also find that the use of the same vocabulary actually hides a variety of interpretations and a range of practice, while using the same descriptors.

The third consideration is the quality of the contact between the school, the teacher and the agents of external change. It was not only institutional involvement but also the relationship of the individual teacher to the programme that was crucial. The individual's ideology was a factor, but other influences included age, domestic circumstances, career prospects, and access to the programme. This last point is influenced by the nature of the interface between the school and the programme. Perhaps the most important aspect of this is the attitude and response of the headteacher. However, while the pivotal influence of the head is important, what is less clear is how a positive reaction by the school leadership will influence individual teacher practice.

The school

Short Road Junior School is on the outskirts of northern city drawing its children, mainly, from the surrounding council estate. Built in the 1930s, apart from the two external classrooms, it is arranged along a central corridor which helped to separate the five main school classrooms into self-contained units. There had been few staff changes in the years preceding the arrival of the new headteacher and the programme co-ordinator in

September 1986. Before the appointment of the co-ordinator and the probationer, who arrived the following year, the youngest member of staff was thirty-five.

The following accounts are based on conversations with four teachers.

Susan

The appointment of the new headteacher (Susan) coincided with the entry of the school into the programme. The previous headteacher had been in post for seventeen years and although not regarded as innovative by the staff, seems to have been respected. Perhaps this was because he allowed the teachers a great deal of professional independence. Susan was appointed from a deputy headship elsewhere in the authority. She had been the first deputy to have been appointed with the involvement of the present senior adviser and was now the first deputy appointed since he arrived to have become a head. Later, at the start of her second term in post, Susan was to describe the senior adviser as 'the irreplaceable figure' in the programme. At the same time she felt that there was the need for 'fundamental change in school'. Susan was in support of the direction of change in classroom practice and organization sponsored by the programme and was also attracted by the provision of extra resources to promote the 'active school'.

Susan found the first term difficult and by Christmas attested to being very tired and agitated. She felt relationships with most of the staff had been strained and she decided to get 'stuck in' after the holiday. However, a start had been made, especially as a strategy had been developed that involved herself and the co-ordinator (Stephanie) working with the deputy head (John), to provide a model classroom, as an example of the new practice, for others in the school. She had also attempted to use LEA courses and visits to other schools to influence change so as to make classroom organization 'more informal'. The appointment of Stephanie, to whom she felt philosophically close, was important to her long term goals, but because of other staff perceptions they had agreed to 'keep some distance so as not to form a clique' and so hinder progress.

Stephanie

Stephanie had previously been a programme co-ordinator in an inner city school in the first phase of the programme. This had not been, in her view, a successful experience. She believed that there had been 'lack of co-operation', from her former head, with whom she had fallen out. A mutually agreed transfer had been arranged, following discussion with the senior adviser.

When first interviewed she had been in post for a term and although feeling that the school had 'a long way to go' she also thought that there were 'great possibilities'. Stephanie was much happier than in her previous post as she felt she had the support of Susan, with whom she 'shared views', and the advisory teacher who worked closely with the school during this period. Her initial teaching interests had been working in schools where she could make use of her ESL qualification. This had influenced her view of the move to Short Road. Short Road was neither inner city nor in need of an ESL specialist, however, a number of discussions with the newly appointed head, who also came from an inner city school, helped to persuade her that it was an appropriate move.

Agreeing with Susan that Short Road was in need of 'revitalization and transformation' she quickly decided that she would work with her to this purpose. As a young teacher, who had trained at the start of the eighties, and previously worked for what she regarded as a progressive authority in a school in the Midlands, the programme seemed to offer the chance to put into practice her own philosophy. Having been previously rebuffed, Susan and the support services appeared to offer the hope of greater success.

As a young scale-two teacher she was less experienced than all the other members of staff which included two scale-three staff as well as John. Through staff meetings and during the initial phase of working alongside other teachers (she was a support and curriculum development teacher at this time), Stephanie felt the resentment of other members of staff. There was also amongst the staff a 'fear of the unknown', prompted by the change instigated by a 'dynamic new head' and herself. Two factors were important in her understanding of this fear; a lack of recent professional development and the major challenge to previous values and practice caused by the prospect of change. Although Stephanie was aware of the resentment and tried 'keeping my distance' from Susan, one member of staff accused her of 'trying to act like a deputy head'. Stephanie believed this was highlighted by the reluctance of John to become involved in the programme in the first term.

During the autumn Stephanie met twice with Susan out of school. They agreed that progress was slow and an initiative was felt necessary. It was decided, together with their advisory teacher, to create a model classroom, based on the organizational pattern that was being encouraged through the programme. This was to be a catalyst for the change that was needed. John was chosen as the target and his classroom was reorganized, after school one evening, by Susan, Stephanie and the advisory teacher. A pattern of designated work areas was constructed and in the following weeks Susan and Stephanie worked alongside John to carry through the organizational initiative into pedagogic practice. By the middle of the following term Stephanie thought that John was 'attuned and cooperative'.

An interesting factor in the role Stephanie was to play was the view she took of her own accountability. Although directly answerable to Susan she was employed by the programme and therefore had a second focus of accountability. She was in a different position from other members of staff and felt herself to be helping to develop good practice, as defined by the programme. However, what good practice was seemed more difficult to describe. While the programme had stated aims, for Stephanie its central purpose was to make 'education more enriching'. Its approach to teaching/learning could be 'justified as functionally more relevant' and as developing the 'provision of skills and attitudes'.

Eileen

When first interviewed Eileen had been at Short Road for twelve years, six as a permanent part-time teacher and the remainder as a full-time scale-one classteacher. Now over forty, she felt that there was little likelihood of dramatic career advancement in the years to come.

The initial staff meeting with Susan gave her some understanding of the change that was to develop during the autumn. The potential change was welcomed as 'a relief'. She had become increasingly depressed by an 'inability to change' that was present in the school. However, she felt the staff as a whole did not welcome the new head as they had been 'well suited by the old regime' and that there was a general fear of the past being questioned. Her initial feelings about what was to come were reinforced by a staff meeting with the senior adviser. This indicated the direction in which the programme was going, especially in regard to teaching style. Eileen described Short Road's style to be 'formal' with good teaching equated to controlled, silent classes. To the staff the impact of the teaching styles recommendations was 'like a bomb'. While herself regarding the changes as a 'great challenge', she felt that the speed and degree of change was 'too much for most of the staff'.

By December of the first term, group work had taken over from class-based 'chalk and talk' as her main organizational form. This had developed through a number of stages so that at this point she organized activity areas around which mixed ability groups rotated. Support in these moves came from Susan and Stephanie, as well as from visits by the advisory teacher.

A year later Eileen, while continuing with group work, still felt Short Road to be 'very insular' with 'closed classrooms' in which she had little idea of what others were doing. Her perception was of little cooperation between staff although some staff were now resigned to change while others now seemed to welcome it. Impending legislation indicated that the recent changes might be reversed by national policy. Eileen was also concerned about the demands of the changes. She felt it to be 'my hardest time in teaching', 'I think everybody is shattered . . . people in general find it hard work (the new teaching style and classroom organization) . . . it's easier to teach something to the whole class'. Eileen felt there to be much more preparation involved now than previously, and alongside this a greater attention to special needs had led to a much bigger burden. A questioning of the new approach also surfaced around parental expectations; parents wanted '. . . results and traditional standards and they always will'.

Throughout this period the senior adviser was seen as a major influence. 'He is present in school through Susan' and he 'was conniving change'. However Susan was a 'nice sort of person' and that although the new orthodoxy was advocated, 'people only change outwardly'. Eileen also thought that colleagues felt that change had been foisted upon them especially through the use of extra resources and the pending building changes. For instance the provision of shared areas in the new re-designed school was seen as 'non-negotiable' and they were 'the biggest factor in the proposed change' and would lead to the sharing of groups of children between teachers.

Eileen who had appeared stimulated and welcomed the prospects of change, the year before, was now thinking of leaving teaching.

John

John had been at Short Road, as deputy head, for seven years. He had taught at a number of other schools in the area and was well regarded by colleagues. He had been acting head for a term following the former head's retirement at Easter. He had also been interviewed for the permanent position. By the following February he showed no obvious resentment toward Susan, and displayed support for the changes that were taking place.

As acting head he had been aware of the programme and the possibility of an extra member of staff in the new school year. However, he had decided to leave any associated planning to the arrival of Susan. Indeed he only began to feel the possible impact of the programme at the staff meeting, the day before the start of term in September. Susan explained the programme, which John saw as 'a major challenge' following the previous seventeen years, when the head 'was not interested in change and had not wanted to become involved'. Indeed, he thought that the school would have been included in the first phase of the programme, if the head had been thought capable of implementing it. This he believed had led to the withholding of resources, until such time as a head, who would make the necessary changes, was in place. From September the impact was great, largely because of the two new members of staff, Susan and Stephanie, who, along with advisers and advisory teachers, were making 'drastic changes, very quickly'.

While, pre-September, John saw staff morale as being low, there was now a chance for 'a complete upgrading' which would go 'hand in glove with good practice'. This was to involve a major re-furbishment of the school as well as the extra resources which were now coming into school.

His own classroom had become, with the help of Susan, Stephanie and the advisory team, 'an example of good practice' and the other teachers had been given time to come into his class, in order to generalize this example. This model was supported by LEA courses, in which the same message was coming from advisers about the direction in which primary practice should be going.

Discussion

In September 1986, change at Short Road Junior was stimulated by the appointment of two key figures and inclusion in the programme. The headteacher and the co-ordinator appeared to share an approach to primary practice that was also the policy of LEA advisers and advisory teachers. This agreement was important to the appointment of Susan and Stephanie, the senior adviser was also the pastoral adviser for the school.

Change took place within the context of increased staffing and the provision of extra resources, later to be supported by an extensive re-design and refurbishment of the school. The impact on the school was dramatic. The professionality of the experienced staff was threatened. Perhaps it is important to discuss this, as it may be thought that the programme encouraged teachers to improve practice, through an examination of their own teaching. To a certain extent, for some of the staff, this was probably true. It seems likely that after initial doubts (not stated by John, but remarked on by other members of staff) John became an acceptor. To a greater or lesser extent this was true of other members of the staff, yet, as we can see in the case of Eileen, this acceptance was not always total or at best can be seen as a pragmatic reaction to the new orthodoxy, as promoted by the authority and key members of staff.

Whether the teachers had profoundly changed, is more difficult to assess. Although a lot of discussion took place, over an extended period, this was around a given notion of good practice. That ideologically this notion was agreed by Susan and Stephanie and later, to one degree or another, by other members of the staff, is important. However, the effect may well have been that one set of operational beliefs was, at least superficially, replaced by another. There are positive aspects to this process. Isolated, static practice which characterized the school before 1986 was challenged. However, there was little attempt to evaluate previous practice, or to identify strengths of individual teachers within the school as a whole.

Although the change process was approached with great concern and care by Susan, the dominant belief which she and other key figures encouraged was that there was a form of practice which was to be developed and that was in itself not open to debate. That the approach adopted to primary practice, when well implemented, has many positive features, is not so much the point. The message to the staff was that their previous practice was effectively redundant. A school staff, which thought itself to have been reasonably successful, was seriously challenged on an ideological level without being encouraged to identify and examine its own values and practices.

For reasons discussed above a technical procedural approach to the implementation of change was adopted. The individual teacher was put in the position, not of the engaged professional, but as implementer, as deliverer. The pedagogic approach of the policy makers, who defined good practice, appears to be radically different from the positions taken by those who are usually identified with this view of teachers as skilled artisans. However, the deskilling (Braverman, 1974) effects may have been similar, especially when the new orthodoxy was shown to be fallible.

The parts of the conversations related are not complete and do not, in themselves, support the argumentation. Most of the conversations did not focus on issues specific to the initiative, which had initiated the research interest. For long periods, especially after a relationship had been established, the concerns were reframed so as to start with the teacher rather than with the programme. Perhaps this helped my own movement from concern with the implementation of the initiative, to that of professional practice in the deeper context of the teachers' lives; to move away from a rationalistic, three-dimensional, theoretical construct (policy, implementation, practice) to a multi or rather complex understanding of the issues. Any attempt to unravel these complexities, through conversation, is riddled with problems of audience, focus and interpretation.

Generalizations, other than those which relate to the complexities of the relationship of teacher to practice, have not been suggested. Furthermore, it is a possible that generalizations founded on empirical observation, standardized surveys and structured interviews are of limited value in giving understanding of what is going on in practice (see, for example; Galton and Simon, 1980; Bennett, 1976). The understanding of practice needs to recognize the complexity and the arbitrariness of the research venture. However, it would be wrong to interpret from this a rejection of macro-influences, rather to acknowledge the intricate nature of the interface with schools and teachers. Nevertheless, educational policy leaders should be encouraged to help teachers 'shatter the structured silence surrounding their teaching', (Smyth, 1989, p. 234), and to resist the temptation to develop a bureaucratic rationality (McTaggart, 1989), which stifles the growth of critical pedagogy.

The research took place during a period of educational centralization, the establishment of the National Curriculum and within the context of a functional view of education, held by national policy makers. At this time there may have been the overtones of a counter ideology, with resonances that had important influences on teachers' disposition and practices. There also came to be a confusion of goals caused by a tightening of central policy on content, while an essentially process-led strategy was being developed at local level.

References

ALEXANDER, R.J. (1984) *Primary Teaching*, London, Holt, Rinehart and Winston.
BENNETT, N. (1976) *Teaching Styles and Pupil Progress*, London, Open Books.
BRAVERMAN, H. (1974) 'Labour and Monopoly Capital', *Monthly Review Press*.
GALTON, M. and SIMON, B. (Eds.) (1980) *Progress and Performance in the Primary Classroom*, London, Routledge and Kegan Paul.
GOODSON, I.F. (1991) 'Sponsoring the Teacher's Voice: Teachers' Lives and Teacher Development', *Cambridge Journal of Education*, **21**, 1.
HARGREAVES, A. (1992) 'Curriculum Reform and the Teacher', *The Curriculum Journal*, **2**, 3.
LAWN, M. (1991) 'Social Constructions of Quality in Teaching', *Evaluation and Research in Education*, **5**, 1 and 2.
McTAGGART, R. (1989) 'Bureaucratic Rationality and the Self-educating Profession: The Problem of Teacher Privatism', *Journal of Curriculum Studies*, **21**, 4.
REYNOLDS, J. and SAUNDERS, M. (1987) 'Teacher Responses to Curriculum Policy: Beyond the "Delivery" Metaphor', in CALDERHEAD, J., *Exploring Teachers Thinking*, London, Cassell.
SCHON, D.A. (1983) *The Reflective Practitioner: How Professionals Think in Action*, New York, Basic Books.
SMYTH, J. (1989) 'Administrative Leadership in the Intellectual Transformation of Schooling', in HOLLY, M.S. and McLOUGHLIN, C.S., *Perspectives on Teacher Professional Development*, London, The Falmer Press.
TOMLINSON, P. (1990) 'Introductory paper', *Conference on the Role of Psychology in Initial Teacher Training*.
WINKLEY, D. (1985) *Diplomats and Detectives*, London, Robert Royce.

12 Changing Classroom Practice Through Teacher Research

Graham Vulliamy and Rosemary Webb

> After I studied my own behaviour in the library, I looked on that of the children with new insight. What had seemed like aimless movement was perhaps simply an intelligent reaction to the realities of the situation, and the gradual breakdown of behaviour and growth of boredom a natural reaction to frustration. (Gregson, 1990, p. 42)

Through working alongside children in a primary school class on the tasks they were set, and discussing these with them as part of an action research project, Gregson describes her developing understanding of what was involved in children finding information in library books. The few edited collections of research done by teachers (for example, Ainscow, 1989; Lomax, 1991a; Webb, 1990) — much of which was conducted in the context of an award-bearing course — demonstrate the potential of teacher research to contribute to teachers' professional development and to effect changes in classroom practice.

There have been very few systematic research enquiries as yet, which aim to investigate the relationships between teacher research and changes in school practice using a broad sample of teacher researchers. The impetus for the study reported here developed from an earlier small-scale research project based upon tape-recorded interviews with each of the eighteen teachers completing the first University of York Outstation MA Programme in Cleveland (UK) 1983–85 (see Webb, 1988). The programme, which consists of part-time and research-based courses of two years' duration, has since been completed by a further eleven cohorts from a variety of LEAs. The aim of the programme is to enable teachers to address their own concerns and the practical problems of their schools within the context of a higher degree. Teachers are recruited in teams and their proposed research projects are supported by their headteachers. The courses are sponsored by LEAs, they are taught in local teachers' centres and supervisions are conducted in participants' schools.

The main aim of the research was to investigate whether and in what ways teacher-research enquiries, conducted in the context of an award-bearing course, might contribute to the processes of professional development, and to change within schools. Data were mainly collected by a combination of questionnaires to all past students and follow-up tape-recorded in-depth interviews. While the research as a whole provided information on the personal and professional benefits and disadvantages of teacher research for individual teachers and its effects on school and LEA policy (Vulliamy and Webb, 1991, 1992a), in this chapter we are concentrating on the kinds of teacher research promoted by the programme and its influence on classroom practice. We acknowledge that our data-base, although detailed and extensive, is open to the criticism that, in the absence of extended observations, it may tend to reproduce the rhetoric rather than the reality of change. However, we believe that in order to understand the effects of forms of INSET on the change process in schools it is vital to listen to the views and experiences of those for whom it is designed.

Approaches to research on the Outstation course

A research methods course consisting of seminars, workshops and discussion groups runs one evening a week throughout the first year of the course. A forum for the discussion of research issues in the second year is provided by voluntary support group meetings led by course tutors, and termly weekend workshops. Through these, teachers are introduced to three broad research approaches — case study, action research and evaluation — together with the kinds of data collection techniques (such as interviewing, classroom observation and document analysis) associated with them. When teaching the course we have found that teachers can more readily differentiate between these approaches if we use a definition of action research, such as Elliott's (1981), which requires at least one full cycle of the action-research spiral being carried out and written up in their theses. This cycle involves reviewing the area or issue to be studied, diagnosing the problems, planning a solution, implementing that solution and monitoring the effects.

Following MacDonald and Walker (1975), we use case study more broadly as an approach which, through the detailed portrayal of 'an instance in action' (p. 2), offers the researcher the possibility of gaining in-depth insights into an area of personal interest or acknowledged difficulty without the requirement that change should occur. On the Outstation course the main distinction made between case-study research and evaluation is that the latter is viewed as explicitly involving the collection of data to evaluate a school event, a new course, policy or innovation. Using the above definitions, case study was found to be by far the most popular with course members. Since we also found that a high percentage of teachers hoped to bring about change by their research, it might be expected that more of them would adopt a model of action research where changes in practice are built into the research process.

Teachers' comments suggest that the reason this does not occur is because there is insufficient time during the two years of the course to work through the action-research cycle. Some teachers who were very clear about their research focus from the outset used an early pilot study required of them during the first year of the course to complete the initial stage of the cycle (for example, Winter, 1990). However, often the nature of the original 'problem' turned out to be much more complex than expected and consequently required more rigorous data collection and analysis than they had originally anticipated (turning the enquiry into a case study rather than just the first phase of an action-research cycle). For example, Peake (1992) intended to develop, implement and monitor a motor programme for one or more of the pupils with cerebral palsy in her class. However, during the timescale of the course she found that she only had time to carry out a general survey of the challenges and difficulties school life posed for these pupils and an in-depth study of the needs of one, for whom she designed a programme.

Action-research projects, which are school or LEA sponsored and where teachers feel under pressure to bring about changes in practice within a specific timescale, may lead to time and effort being put into planning and implementing changes at the expense of data collection and analysis. Also, action-research projects led by a member of the school's senior management, which emphasize the action rather than the research, run the risk of becoming a manipulative device to justify and implement prespecified changes with little or no modification to existing plans or increased understanding of the issues. In a higher degree context, where there is an increasing expectation that theses will demonstrate methodological rigour and grounded theorizing, theses based on an inadequate research base are likely to fail — thereby reinforcing theory/practice divide which action research was designed to bridge. For example, the research of a secondary deputy head into pupil profiling, which while it was extremely successful in bringing about change in recordkeeping and reporting to parents throughout his school, gave rise to a thesis where the claims made were insufficiently substantiated, resulting in its referral. By contrast, case-study research gives the teacher researcher more space for in-depth data collection and critical reflection, thus providing a greater opportunity to meet academic criteria. Our findings also suggest that case study as a research approach for teachers has considerable potential for leading to changes (but usually after the completion of the research) because of the greater understanding of the likely need for, and nature of, possible changes brought about by systematic and detailed enquiry. For example, Wright (1990) carried out a case study of her use of the language of mathematics with her infant

class. The process of examining the data in detail and consulting the literature about emerging issues led her to seek ways of enabling the children
both to understand and to use new mathematical vocabulary. She also
tried to increase her repertoire of questioning techniques to encourage them
to reason and to speculate.

In the context of INSET to meet special educational needs, Ainscow
and Hart (1992) discuss the differing perspectives on the change process
underpinning alternative types of INSET and the role of the 'outsider' INSET
providers. They define the role of the 'outsider' in teacher research as 'to
support the process of enquiry and then contribute to an explanation of
findings and the formulation of possible responses' (p. 118). However,
they are increasingly concerned that, in relation to teacher research,

> for some, our lack of imposition of particular interpretations and
> approaches may seem disconcertingly lacking in direction; our
> insistence that teachers need to define and determine their own
> solutions may be experienced as a failure to provide adequate
> content, input, 'examples of practice' and so on (p. 119).

They go on to explore a way forward where course members and tutors
make their values and experiences explicit as a resource in context which
they hope will allow equal status to the perspectives of all participants.

The Outstation programme has certain corporate values implicit in the
course aims and pedagogy which convey messages that it serves to promote broadly 'progressive' classroom practices. Individual tutors may experience the tensions described by Ainscow and Hart when they supervise
teachers carrying out investigations in the particular area of expertise for
which they are known, although the diversity of teacher-research projects
on the Outstation Programme means this happens relatively infrequently.
However, central to developing teacher-research tradition at the University
of York is the notion that changes in practice as a result of the programme
will be based upon insights derived from critical reflection on evidence.
What constitutes an improvement is to be defined by the teachers. Therefore,
the programme places considerable time and emphasis on introducing
teachers, through practical work geared to their enquiries, to the processes
involved in the rigorous collection, analysis and validation of data.

Winter (1992), in his review of McKernan's 'handbook of methods and
resources for the reflective practitioner' poses the question 'what is the
relationship between practitioners', reflection upon their practice and lists
of social-science-based investigative techniques?' (p. 115). We have found
that the use of these techniques — notably semi-structured interviews and
participant observation — gives teachers data to reflect on to which they
would otherwise not have gained access, and leads them to look afresh at
the all-too-familiar in their classrooms and question the taken-for-granted.
Through the process of grappling with the meaning of the data many

teachers come to a deeper understanding of the ambiguity and complexity of the issues that are the subject of their projects and in some cases develop critiques of the macro-context of their practices. However, while the course introduces teachers to some of the data collection and analysis techniques of the social sciences, it also encourages them to develop their own approaches. Examples of such individual approaches include McCann's (1990) use of an unattended video camera, Peake's (1992) use of parent diaries and Gregson (1990) analyzing her own response to a task set for the class, as illustrated in the opening extract to this chapter. Regular workshops for supervisors help to promote a consistent approach to facilitating teachers' research.

The importance attached to the research process, which has led to the Programme being criticized as 'traditional' (Lomax, 1991c), contrasts with some teacher-research traditions where the emphasis is upon improving practice through changing the values and perspectives of teachers. Thus, for example, Whitehead (1989) advocates the use of video to highlight for teachers the 'living contradictions' of their values in action; Griffiths and Tann (1991) consider a range of techniques, such as the use of images and metaphor, to help uncover teachers' 'personal theories'; and Lomax (1991b) discusses the importance of 'critical friends' in examining teachers' claims about their professional development and the relationship between their values and educational change. To varying degrees teachers on the Outstation programme embark upon a process of personal self-scrutiny. This comes about through questions raised by Outstation course exercises — for example, one involving teams interpreting photographs of each other's schools to reveal the multiple interpretations of evidence and the reasons for this — and the data that teachers collect for their research projects. They may choose to reflect on, explore and challenge their beliefs and ideologies privately or seek the support of their tutor and/or their team colleagues. For example, Gregson (1990) describes how her research led to a fundamental questioning of her beliefs and practices which was initially very threatening and deskilling and the way in which in order to move forward she needed support from both her team colleagues and her supervisor. However, there is no requirement that the teachers' research should lead them into this arena and subsequently when it happens it is through choice and personal commitment to self-evaluation.

Changing perspectives on practice

Sometimes changes in practice that occurred were as a result of course exercises — for example, the re-organization of some of the work areas around an infant school following a headteacher's observations of the nature and frequency of their use for a research assignment. Teachers' research also sometimes brought about unintended changes in areas related, but not central to, their studies. For example, as part of her research into managing support work in the primary classroom, a teacher and her colleagues carried out a week's survey of the incidence and nature of the involvement of 'extra' people in their classrooms. An incidental factor to emerge was the high number of interruptions to which classes were subjected. This finding gave rise to much comment in the staffroom and a commitment by the headteacher and staff not to send children around the school during lesson time with lost property and non-urgent enquiries and requests.

Involvement in the teacher-research process was also viewed as bringing about change in the attitudes of colleagues, who were not enrolled on the course. Course members described how interview questions raised interviewees' awareness of issues, and feedback from classroom observations challenged assumptions: 'When we sought people's views on assessment methods used in the school, some teachers decided that there were inadequacies in their methods and they were going to make changes'. (Questionnaire)

The research process was also regarded as a vehicle for improving staff relationships by giving the researcher a reason and an opportunity to discover other teachers' points of view and therefore to take a more co-operative approach to decision-making: 'I was listening to other staff and I was listening to pupils and it was the research that made me listen far more to other people than I had actually done before'. (Interview)

Where opportunities could be created for teachers to observe in colleagues' classrooms these generated valuable data for understanding classroom interactions. Farrell (1992) in his study of meeting individual needs in a comprehensive school classroom describes how through his observations he came to appreciate the nature of the often threatening and unrealistic demands staff unwittingly placed on children with moderate learning difficulties and their resultant coping strategies which he and his colleagues found so disruptive. Following analysis of the observations through interviews with support staff, he was able to draw on their experience and ideas in order to recommend teaching approaches to improve the situation for both pupils and teachers.

The interview data suggested that a major effect of the research on the practice of course members was in their changed attitudes towards their pupils and the value that they came to ascribe to their views. On re-checking the questionnaire data, we found that over half the sample had obtained data from pupils. This data gave teachers insights at first hand into the dichotomy between the rhetoric and the reality of classroom practice and the curriculum as intended by the teacher and experienced by the pupil. For example, a secondary head of a Communications Faculty, who observed in a range of classrooms and talked to staff, found that 'an incredible discrepancy really does happen and I think from my point of view I've been quite surprised at what classrooms are about'. A major finding of his research was the manner in which pupils frequently act as interpreters of teachers' talk to other pupils. This realization led him both to try to improve teacher-pupil and pupil-pupil interactions in his own lessons, and to use his research findings to raise the level of awareness of factors promoting and constraining communication within his faculty.

In some cases pupil data had led to a major reassessment of pupils' abilities. For example, in an action-research project, one primary class teacher recorded the children's discussion in science as they worked in collaborative groups. She had her expectations of pupils' achievements challenged by the data:

> One thing that I was quite stunned by was the ability of some children, who you would class as having learning difficulties and the contribution that they made in the working groups. . . . One of the boys, who went for special remedial reading lessons, quite clearly in his group was organizing the work and coming up with some very good ideas and questioning a lot of what was happening . . . I thought well this isn't right, if a child has this ability and I haven't recognized it. (Interview)

She described how she learned about teaching through groupwork from the process of collecting and reflecting on the data, which involved visiting a science co-ordinator in another school, keeping a diary, the observations of her classroom by her tutor and a colleague, taping groupwork and interviewing pupils. The data continuously generated ideas to be tested out and refined in her classroom. As the project progressed, her changed approach to science teaching began to affect her classroom organization and teaching style in other curriculum areas.

Factors facilitating and constraining change

Open-ended questions in the questionnaires revealed that the major factor facilitating change was thought to be involvement in the research process. Critical reflection on data — especially that derived from pupils — led staff to question their existing beliefs and practices and to try out alternative ideas. Fortuitous timing was cited as the second most important factor assisting change. This was particularly in relation to projects which addressed pressing whole-school concerns — such as one on truancy — or reflected national initiatives, notably TVEI and the implementation of the National Curriculum core subjects. Thus, an acting head of a secondary school was able to use his study of teaching primary science, which involved teacher and pupil interviews and classroom observations in twenty feeder schools, as a basis for INSET within the catchment area.

The support of the headteacher was identified as the third most important factor enabling changes to take place. On a practical level, teachers referred to the various ways in which heads had given them time and opportunities to conduct their research during school hours. Supportive heads also demonstrated an ongoing interest and commitment to the research and facilitated the communication of research findings to the rest of the staff:

> At each stage when I thought that I'd learned something or discovered something, I shared it with him (the head) and we discussed it and really, because he gave me such a lot of freedom in what I was doing, I was able to put into practice the things that came out. He used it as a staff development exercise, as a curriculum development exercise generally, which was very good. (Interview)

An open-ended question in the questionnaires asking for factors that prevented changes resulting from the teachers' research suggested that there were three main barriers to change: moving schools during the course or shortly after its completion; the pressure of other innovations; and lack of time. For those promoted during the course, the work associated with their new role often had detrimental effects on the progress of the research and the writing up of the thesis. Generally the changes instigated by the researchers ceased or were short-lived when those responsible moved on; however, occasionally where the findings were valued the changes were taken up by others.

Outstation initiatives were usually only one of several innovations making demands on staff. Lack of time owing to the pressure of other school commitments and the need to become involved in the implementation of additional innovations were common constraints on the conduct of the research. New national initiatives which suddenly became school priorities or contributed to 'innovation overload' were frequently viewed as reducing staff time and interest and their inclination to participate in the research.

Influencing practice throughout the school

A common theme in the literature on educational change is the difficulty of translating individual change into more widespread changes affecting other teachers and wider school processes. To move from changes in the classroom practice of individuals to wider changes in practice throughout the school requires that the lessons learned from an individual's research are shared in some way with a wider audience within the school or LEA.

For many, the research seemed to be viewed as a very private enterprise:

> I mean really I think my research has stayed fairly private. A lot of other staff in school I don't think are aware of what went on. There was no real report back to the other staff as to what had happened, so it was only people who were actually involved with me who were really familiar with it. (Interview)

Other research suggests that schools are characterized by this very private and individualized approach to teaching (e.g. Nias, 1989, pp. 169–70). An American study has found that teacher researchers operating within this prevailing school culture characterized by individualism and hierarchical decision-making developed their own counter-culture to support their activities. Some British studies have also found a tendency for groups of teacher-researchers to work together to ignore or subvert school norms and Elliott views the kind of self-generating critical pedagogy associated with action research as providing 'a form of creative resistance to the hegemony of the state' (1991, p. 117).

Our data did contain a few references to individuals, whose changed perceptions made them feel alienated from colleagues, and many comments on staff indifference to the research, which was often attributed to lack of time and other commitments. However, we found no evidence of teams forming a counter-culture or trying to work outside the school system. Possible explanations for this are that teachers felt a certain loyalty to schools that had supported their application and those, who viewed course participation as a means of career enhancement, would be unlikely to work actively to undermine the intentions of senior management. The evidence does suggest that teachers tried, with differing degrees of success, to work within and influence school cultures. Staff counter-cultures by their very nature are marginalized from the main avenues of decision-making and from the individuals which they most seek to influence. Consequently, teacher research seems likely to be a more effective means of changing policy and practice in a school if it can become fundamental to the ways of thinking and acting of all its members and valued by those in power positions.

Our research illustrates the importance of what Nias *et al.* (1989) refer to as a 'collegial' school culture, where sharing is actively encouraged, and supports Evans and Hopkins' (1988) view that a more democratic school climate facilitates the uptake of new ideas. An illustration of this is McCann's (1990) research into the culture of Mirpuri children, which had a considerable impact on both policy and practice in the school in which she worked. In an interview with her it became clear that the school climate was such that the head actively encouraged her to share her findings and all the staff in the infant school except the new deputy head read her thesis.

Our findings also generally endorse the increasing body of literature which argues that for teacher research to effect changes in classroom practice throughout the school, then the culture of the school must be one which values critical reflection on evidence and the sharing of ideas. However, we believe that this recent emphasis upon changing school organization and culture can be overplayed, as, for example, in Hopkins' contention that 'it is very difficult to change education — even in a single classroom — without also changing the school organization' (1989, p. 84). The data reveal the potential of the research process to develop teachers' confidence and ability to take action both within and beyond their own classroom. This suggests that it is impossible to divorce educational improvement from increased understanding of classroom interaction and the learning process; or to separate a school's institutional growth and change from the professional development and changing attitudes and practices of those that make up the institution.

References

AINSCOW, M. (Ed.) (1989) *Special Education in Change*, London, David Fulton.

AINSCOW, M. and HART, S. (1992) 'Moving practice forward', *Support for Learning*, August.

ELLIOTT, J. (1981) *Action-Research: A Framework for Self-Evaluation in Schools*, Cambridge, Schools Council 'Teacher-Pupil Interaction and the Quality of Learning' Project, Working Paper No. 1.

ELLIOTT, J. (1991) *Action-Research for Educational Change*, Milton Keynes, Open University Press.

EVANS, M. and HOPKINS, D. (1988) 'School climate and the psychological state of the individual teacher as factors affecting the utilisation of educational ideas following an inservice course', *British Educational Research Journal*, **14**, 3, pp. 211–230.

FARRELL, T. (1992) 'Meeting individual needs in the classroom in a comprehensive school', in VULLIAMY, G. and WEBB, R. (Eds.) *Teacher Research and Special Educational Needs*, London, David Fulton.

GREGSON, D. (1990) 'Why do pirates have peg legs? A study of reading for information', in WEBB, R. (Ed.) *Practitioner Research in the Primary School*, London, Falmer Press.

GRIFFITHS, M. and TANN, S. (1991) 'Ripples in the reflection', in LOMAX, P. (Ed.) *Managing Better Schools and Colleges: An Action Research Way*, Multilingual Matters.

HOPKINS, D. (1989) 'Identifying INSET Needs: A School Improvement perspective', in McBRIDE, R. (Ed.) *The In-Service Training of Teachers*, London Falmer Press.

LOMAX, P. (Ed.) (1991a) *Managing Better Schools and Colleges: An Action Research Way*, Multilingual Matters.

LOMAX, P. (1991b) 'Peer review and action research', in LOMAX, P. (Ed.) *Managing Better Schools and Colleges: An Action Research Way*. Multilingual Matters.

LOMAX, P. (1991c) 'Review of Practitioner Research in the Primary School', *Educational Review*, **43**, pp. 371–2.

McCann, A. (1990) 'Culture and behaviour, a study of Mirpuri Pakistani infant pupils', in Webb, R. (Ed.) *Practitioner Research in the Primary School*, London, Falmer Press.

MacDonald, B. and Walker, R. (1975) 'Case-study and the social philosophy of educational research', *Cambridge Journal of Education*, **5**, pp. 2–11.

Nias, J. (1989) *Primary Teachers Talking*, London, Routledge and Kegan Paul.

Nias, J. *et al.* (1989) *Staff Relationships in the Primary School*, London, Cassell.

Peake, L. (1992) 'Devising motor programmes for children with physical disabilities', in Vulliamy, G. and Webb, R. (Eds.) *Teacher Research and Special Educational Needs*, London, David Fulton.

Vulliamy, G. and Webb, R. (1991) 'Teacher research and educational change: An empirical study', *British Educational Research Journal*, **17**, pp. 219–36.

Vulliamy, G. and Webb, R. (1992a) 'The influence of teacher research: Process or product?', *Educational Review*, 44, pp. 41–58.

Vulliamy, G. and Webb, R. (1992b) *Teacher Research and Special Educational Needs*, London, David Fulton.

Webb, R. (1988) 'Out-station teams: A collaborative approach to research in schools', *British Educational Research Journal*, 14, pp. 51–64.

Webb, R. (Ed.) (1990) *Practitioner Research in the Primary School*, London, Falmer Press.

Whitehead, J. (1989) 'Creating a living educational theory from questions of the kind "How do I improve my practice?"', *Cambridge Journal of Education*, 19, pp. 41–52.

Winter, R. (1992) 'Review of Curriculum Action Research: A Handbook of Methods and Resources for the Reflective Practitioner', *Cambridge Journal of Education*, 22, pp. 114–15.

Winter, V. (1990) 'A process approach to science', in Webb, R. (Ed.) *Practitioner Research in the Primary School*, London, Falmer Press.

Wright, S. (1990) 'Language counts in the teaching of mathematics', in Webb, R. (Ed.) *Practitioner Research in the Primary School*, London, Falmer Press.

Notes on Contributors

Philip Adey is a Senior Lecturer in Science Education the Centre for Educational Studies, King's College London. Work with science curriculum development in Britain and overseas and the exploration of ways to help pupils develop higher order thinking has led him into a concern with the factors which lead to change in classrooms. At Kings's he is heavily involved in INSET and increasingly worried about the long-term effectiveness of the INSET that providers deliver.

Alison Bishop is a Senior Lecturer in Early Childhood Studies with Science at the University of Northumbria at Newcastle. She has had over twenty years experience of teaching children in early-years classrooms. Research interests include young children problem solving, gender dynamics and the place of play in the early-years curriculum.

John Carneson taught in Southern and Eastern Africa before coming to London to teach and study. Recently he has completed a research studentship at the University of Sunderland School of Education. He now lectures at the University of Cape Town, South Africa.

Ray Chatwin, Paul McGowan, Maggie Turner and Trisha Wick were the members of the Schools In-Service Unit of the Ethnic Minority Support Service of Birmingham City Council. Over a number of years their work contributed to the development of whole school responses to a range of development needs.

Hilary Constable is Professor of Education at the School of Education, University of Sunderland. She was formerly a lecturer at the School of Education, University of Leeds and previously at New College, Durham and Middleton St George College of Education. Her research and teaching interests are in the part played in improving schooling by professional and organizational development.

Paul Cooper is a Research Officer in the Department of Education Studies, University of Oxford. He taught for ten years before becoming a full-time educational researcher in 1989. His research interests include behavioural problems in schools, effective schools, and more recently effective teaching and learning. He is particularly interested in participants' (especially pupils') perspectives on schooling. He has published on all of these areas of interest. His most recent major publication is *Effective Schools for Disaffected Students* (Routledge, 1993).

Marion Dadds is Tutor in Educational Studies at the University of Cambridge Institute of Education. She teaches on a variety of in-service courses, mostly with primary teachers. Her main professional interests include the role of research-based in-service work in teacher and school development; the felt experience of being a change agent; links between teacher action research and teacher appraisal. Marion's current concerns include the role of topic work in the primary National Curriculum, English in the primary years and the primary school as an ethical institution. Job satisfaction is at its highest for her when in-service teachers become excited by their own discoveries, as they research their classroom practice.

Thomas Dalton is a Visiting Lecturer, University of Greenwich and an Open University tutor for the MA (Education) and PGCE programmes. Previous experience includes teaching in London primary and comprehensive schools, a lectureship at Avery Hill College, Co-director of the Schools Council Geography for the Young School Leaver Project 1970–74, and Senior Tutor for the B Ed. (Hons) In-Service degree at Thames Polytechnic. In 1985 he was awarded a doctorate by the University of Leicester. He is co-author of *Fieldwork in Geography* (Batsford, 1968), and author of *The Challenge of Curriculum Innovation* (Falmer Press, 1988).

Steve Farrow is a Principal Lecturer in the School of Education at the University of Sunderland. His responsibilities include the coordination of Primary Science Education, and his principal individual research interest relates to the impact of the requirements of the National Curriculum on science education in primary classrooms.

John Harland is Head of NFER's Northern Office. He gained a first degree with the Open University. Having taught in secondary, primary and special schools, he lectured on education in various Higher Education institutions. After taking a D.Phil at the University of York, he undertook research into the early career experiences of college graduates and then joined the NFER in 1984. He has completed several national and local evaluation projects, including studies of lower-attaining pupils in secondary schools, INSET and the arts.

Kay Kinder is a Senior Research Officer at NFER Northern Office. She worked for ten years as a primary teacher, and from 1985 has worked full time in research and evaluation. Having been research fellow on the central team of the Primary Needs Independent Evaluation Project (PRINDEP). She joined NFER in 1989. Since then, she has carried out a range of local and national case-study evaluations, primarily in the field of INSET and the arts.

Donald Mcintyre is Reader in Educational Studies at the University of Oxford. He has been engaged in research on teaching and teacher education over the last thirty years, mostly in Scotland. His most recent publications, both in January 1993, are *Making Sense of Teaching* (Open University Press), with Sally Brown, and *Mentoring* (Kogan Page), which he edited with Hazel Hagger and Margaret Wilkin. His current work with Paul Cooper reflects both a continuing concern to understand teachers' perspectives and a concern to give equal weight to pupils' perspectives.

Peter Millward is a Lecturer in the School of Education at Durham University where he is director designate of the BA (Ed) Course. He teaches language and drama on the undergraduate and post-graduate primary courses, contributes to the MA programme and supervises students working for MA and PhD research degrees. His research interests include INSET evaluation, poetry in primary schools and the language of young children's drama. He is engaged in a variety of INSET initiatives with a focus on storytelling, reading and drama in nursery and primary schools.

Jerry Norton started working on research into curriculum change when a primary teacher in the West Riding of Yorkshire. More recently as a Senior Lecturer at the University of Sunderland he has been working on initial and post-graduate degrees. Current research and publication interests include change in teacher practice, school development planning and school-based support in initial training.

Richard Simpson is a Senior Lecturer in Science and Environmental Education, University of Northumbria at Newcastle, with a wide spectrum of teaching experience from education of young children to work with mature students. Research interests include young children problem solving, gender dynamics and how new technologies affected the North-east Fishing Industry.

Linda Thompson is a Lecturer in Education at the University of Durham where she coordinates the Language and Literacy courses on initial and post-graduate teacher education courses. She has taught in multilingual primary schools in the UK as well as training English teachers at Universities in Holland and Sweden.

Graham Vulliamy is a Senior Lecturer in Educational Studies at the University of York, where he teaches courses on teacher research, sociology of education and education in developing countries. His most recent books are *Doing Educational Research in Developing Countries: Qualitative Strategies* (co-authored with Keith Lewin and David Stephens, Falmer Press, 1990) and *Teacher Research and Special Educational Needs* (co-edited with Rosemary Webb, David Fulton Publishers, 1992).

Rosemary Webb ran the University of York Teacher-Research Outstation MA Programme before becoming a Professional Officer for Primary Education at the National Curriculum Council in 1989. She left the NCC in 1991 to take up a Senior Research Fellowship in the School of Education at the University of Manchester and she is now a part-time Lecturer in that department. She is the editor of *Practitioner Research in the Primary School* (Falmer Press, 1990) and the co-editor (with Graham Vulliamy) of *Teacher Research and Special Educational Needs* (David Fulton Publishers, 1992).

Index